# Master

*A step-by-step guide on how to setup an exceptional campaign*

*In just 3 hours and manage it for just 1 hour a week!*

## Mike Ncube

Cover Design: Abirhasan
Layout Design: Rasel Khondokar
Editor: Nikki Johnson
© 2020 Lulu Author. All rights reserved.
ISBN 978-0-244-26987-6

*' Fantastic Google ads service from Mike '*

*I highly recommend Mike. Mike really does know his stuff when it comes to Google Ads PPC. Mike is very reliable, his communication is great and he always completes work in a speedy manner. I will certainly be using mike again -* **Cut Keys Direct**

*' Let Mike Ncube untangle the tangled web that is Google Ads'*

*Mike took what was to me a mystery, i.e. Google Ads, and formulated a campaign based on the brief I gave him which was right on the button. I noticed an immediate increase in activity on my landing page and from there a steadily increasing flow of appointments made. His weekly reports condense the information so that it is understandable –* **Greg, Kilmarnock Hearing Care.**

*' ROI has improved! '*

*So far so good! Leads are coming in from Mike's management. ROI is improving as the month's roll on. He answers all my emails promptly with great understanding and knowledge of his trade. I'd recommend Mike Ncube to anyone from which I hear needs his expertise –* **Michael, Highland Digital**

*' Easy and Efficient! '*

*Great service by Mike, really easy process. From enquiry to quote was only a few working hours and Mike had audited our account in this time and pin pointed areas on improvement which correlated with that we had been told previously so knew he wasn't just making issues up. Payment was made to Mike and again he was ruthlessly efficient in getting the work done, only a couple of days! Will no doubt be using these services again! –* **Jonny Wright**

*' Superb keep up the good work Mike!! '*

*Mike is a man of talents, exceptional knowledge and world-class service. Been with Mike for 3 months and I am honestly lost for words. He has delivered since day one and the work is evident. The support is amazing and responds to emails as and when he gets it. I would highly recommend to anyone –* **AC Design Solutions**

*' OUTSTANDING - We are fully BOOKED after just one month! '*

*Mike is by far the best PPC consultant I have worked with. He implements FAST, has a real attention to detail, he is technically outstanding with a complete understanding of current Google Ads/analytics tips and tricks. We run a residential Detox centre (the Milestone Detox) and before using Mike we were not ranking with SEO and not getting many PPC leads as a result we were running at 40% to 60% capacity. Within ONE MONTH of using Mike, we are now fully booked 100% capacity for the next 8 weeks! He is OUTSTANDING –* **Jonathan Cavan, Milestone Detox**

*' The search is over after numerous people promising results for my Google Ads ... '*

*The search is over after numerous people promising results for my Google Ads account and not delivering I was fortunate to find Mike Ncube. I am very pleased with the campaign had loads of calls and enquiries could not recommend enough!!! –* **Anthony Dunn**

*' Insightful and actionable consultation '*

*Mike gave me a very insightful and actionable consultation on our new Google Ads campaign. He was very friendly and accommodating to go over some additional advice over the phone. He not only covered the basics of a campaign but gave numerous useful hints and tips which have already had an impact on our sales. I would highly recommend Mike to set-up or advise on your Google Ads campaign –* **Tom Eastman**

*' Excellent work promptly carried out '*

*Mike quickly understood our business and requirements, producing a Google Ads campaign tailored to our needs. A rare find in a service sector where many offer little work for a lot of money –* **Brian S.**

*' Excellent knowledge on Google Ads and Supportive '*

*Mike is an excellent person to work with! I was very happy with his Google Ads setup for my travel biz. He is very supportive and always ready to clear your queries, which I found very important for a curious person like me. I have already contracted him for the monthly management of Google Ads. Now looking for the results!! –* **Vikas Agarwal**

*' Our 'go to' man for Google Ads '*

*Over the last few years we use Mike as our 'go to' man for Google Ads. His attention to detail and ability to interpret our flaky briefs has always given us the confidence to stick with him. We are a small design agency and sometimes need whole Google Ads accounts set-up or just minor updates to existing accounts. Mike responds quickly and doesn't seem concerned how big or small the job might be. Highly recommend! –* **Ed in Midlands**

# CONTENTS

# Foreword

Congratulations on taking the first step to running effective Google Ads campaigns. You won't regret it!

Google Ads is the premier pay per click advertising (PPC) platform for businesses looking to advertise online. Whether it's a product, service, business or event, Google Ads is the ideal platform to launch and promote it.

Like many advertisers, you probably don't have the funds to employ an expert and you've already spent all your marketing budget on your advertising campaigns. So learning the Google Ads system to set up and manage your campaigns is a priority.

Anyone can set up an exceptional Google Ads campaign with the right information. Whether you're a busy plumber with little advertising knowledge, or you run an SME with a growing team, you can now set up and manage effective campaigns with no prior knowledge.

Many books and tutorials show you the features and tools in Google Ads - and stop there. They don't show you how the experts actually do it. This guide will take you through the process used by a leading Google Ads expert and you'll learn how to manage it for just 1 hour a week, with no prior knowledge.

This book is for beginners and regular users alike and anyone with responsibility for setting up and managing paid search campaigns in Google Ads.

This also includes:

1. Search marketers that are looking to improve their campaigns

2. Search marketing students with basic knowledge and want more insight

3. Business owners that want to improve their search campaigns and want to sharpen their skills

4. Advertisers with little or no advertising experience and seasoned users.

As a Google Premier Partner, I've worked with many small and medium advertisers and understand how important digital advertising is to their businesses. It represents a big part of reaching their potential customers and engaging them to increase their profitability.

This book is divided into two sections. The first section deals with setting up your campaign; and account if you don't already have one. I walk you through the steps required to launch a campaign and you will understand all the features and controls that are at your disposal in the campaign. This initial setup should take no more than 3 hours to complete.

In section two, your campaign is ready and launched and now you need to manage it. You'll learn why it is important to manage your campaign and not just leave it to run - especially in the first month of launching it. And you'll discover how to do that effectively in just an hour a week.

*Mike Ncube, Google Ads Specialist*

# SECTION ONE

# Introduction

In this section, we will be setting up your account and campaign and the various settings you need to advertise on Google. Our focus will be on setting up a Google search campaign to target people that are searching for your products, services, business, events, and so on. And you should be able to complete this within 3 hours, by following the process in this book.

There are no specific rules for creating a Google Ads campaign and the process can be approached in different ways. However, there are basic tasks that anyone looking to set up an effective campaign should follow.

Google Ads has various campaigns types. Whether you have a website, landing page, app or video that you'd like to promote, this is all possible in Google Ads.

For each, there's a process to follow in setting up the campaign. Following them will help you create targeted ads that convert at a high rate.

Search ads are the primary campaign type in Google Ads. You see search ads when you do a search on Google or one of the search partner sites, and with these, you use keywords related to your products or services to show ads to your target customers.

The process you will follow here you can also use in setting up other campaigns, including campaigns on Microsoft advertising, with a few variations.

So, let's dive in, and set up an exceptional campaign for your business.

# CHAPTER 1

# Setting up your account - 20 minutes

## Introduction

The first step to advertising on Google begins with setting up a Google Ads account. You'll need an account to launch ads that will target people that are looking for your products or services.

In this section, we will cover the different campaign types available to you as an advertiser. Your choice will depend on your goals, the nature of your business, your experience and various other factors.

This part of the setup should only take you 20 minutes to complete. You'll also find out what you need to set up the account and how that will save you time and money in the future.

**Please note:** you may have to set up a dummy campaign initially to get your account ready and to add your billing details. Just remember to pause it. Then you can set up your campaign with instructions from chapter 2 onwards.

## Account Setup

How you set up Google Ads depends on your type of business. If you're an agency that manages client accounts or are a very large advertiser, then you'll likely need a Google Ads Manager Account.

A Manager Account allows you to do the following tasks, all in one login interface:

1. Setup new advertiser accounts

2. Add or remove new users to existing and new accounts

3. Use one login to access all accounts you're managing

4. Easily move from one account to another

5. Assign credit to advertisers' accounts (if you've been approved for credit)

There are two campaign types available to all advertisers. Whether you're an agency creating an account in your

Manager account, or a regular advertiser, you have two account types you can set up:

1. Smart Campaign account (formerly AdWords Express)

2. Google Ads account

The Smart Campaign account is a simplified Google Ads account. It's an automated account so you won't do any bid changes, ad and keyword optimisation or other actions that you do with a normal account.

This account is usually best for people that are completely new to Google Ads and want Google to handle the management. You can also set it up as a test account to assess the returns you get from Google without fully plunging in. It's commonly used by small micro-businesses like florists, plumbers, cafés and other small businesses targeting a local client base.

One of its main benefits is that it takes minutes to fully set up and run. However, this account type is very limited and is almost impossible to scale.

Another benefit is that you don't need a website to advertise with a Smart Campaign account, unlike the main account.

To fully reap the benefits of Google Ads, you should set up using a full Google Ads Account type. This has many benefits, including:

- Full control of bidding tools with automated and manual bidding options
- Full control of text ads and other creatives and makes your ads more prominent
- Access to other campaign types like Video, Shopping and Display, besides search campaigns
- Ability to manage your keywords and match types to control the searches you get
- Advertising inventory of millions of websites to advertise on, and not just Google.com

In this book, I'll walk you through setting up a full Google Ads account and how to set up an effective campaign and manage it.

To set up a full Google Ads account you'll need the following:

1. An email address
2. A website for your business

If you have a Google Account that is linked to other Google products like Gmail, you can use the same email address to set up your account.

All you do is enter the email address and password when you're ready to sign up here: https://www.ads.google.com

Next, you'll add your billing details. You should do this before creating your campaign so you can add the free voucher that's available for new accounts – if you have received one from Google.

**Payment Methods and Billing Options**

When setting up payment settings for your Google Ads account, you'll set up your payment method and billing options.

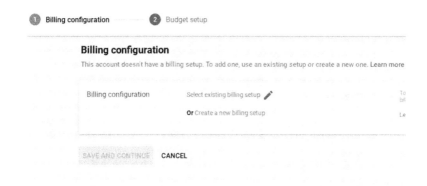

The billing options available to you depend on your country settings. These will be available to you as you set up your account and will determine how you pay.

Choosing the right option will ensure your ads run without any interruption and this could be a big benefit to your account.

## There are three payment setting options in Google Ads:
### Automatic payments

Use this option if you prefer to be automatically charged after your ads run. You are charged every 30 days after your last automatic charge or when you reach a pre-set amount, like £500 (known as your payment threshold), whichever comes first. You can also make a payment at any time to control your costs.

## Manual payments

You should choose this option if you want to have greater control over costs. With this option, you make a payment before your ads run. As your ads run and you accrue costs, the balance in your account will decrease and when it's depleted your ads will stop running. The problem with this option is that you could miss out on some opportunities when your ads are offline.

## Monthly invoicing (credit option)

This option is only available to advertisers that meet certain requirements. This includes large advertisers and agencies that manage accounts for their clients. This means you only get one invoice for all your advertising accounts and you have 30 days to pay the invoice. Payment is made by cheque or bank transfer.

This simplifies billing for large advertisers and means there is no disruption to your ads, like when there is a credit card problem, for example.

Your payment method is what you use to pay your advertising bills, such as credit or debit card. Your choice will depend on your country and the currency that you've selected.

## Google Ads Voucher

For new accounts, Google offers free vouchers to use towards your advertising. At the time of writing, £75 or $75 is the standard voucher they offer. The terms are that if you spend £25 within 30 days of launching your campaign, you'll receive £75 of free advertising.

For your account to be eligible for a voucher, it has to be less than 15 days old.

Google Ads offers a number of vouchers that are available to their partners. There are vouchers for each campaign type: Search, Display and Video. And these are automatically applied to your account when you launch these campaign types.

## The Google Ads Brief

A campaign brief is key to setting up an effective campaign. It outlines the objectives, target audience, budgets, products or services, strategies, and tactics of the campaign.

It's always best to work from a brief. This ensures that you have all you need before starting. This is especially important if you're an agency setting up a client account and need to understand the business better.

If you're setting up your own campaigns, make sure you have everything in hand and create a campaign brief that you can work from. Carry out thorough research into your customers and competitors and include that in the brief.

Look at what they need and how they could benefit from your products and make a list of strong Unique Selling Points (USPs). You'll need these when you create your ads.

At a minimum, you'll need the following information in the brief:

- What is your product or service?

- What is unique about it that will make people want to buy? (USP)

14

- Who would want to buy your product or service?

- Where are they based?

- What would you like them to do when they get to your website? (Goals)

- How much are you willing to spend each month to target them? (Budget)

- Have you thought about a few keywords that will help target your customers?

- Who will you be competing against? (Competitors)

Reviewing the above questions and researching each of them will help you to set up an exceptional campaign.

The last thing you want is for your Ads to look like hundreds of others out there. If they do, you will struggle to differentiate your business and will produce mediocre results.

You will also struggle to outrank competitors. Appearing at the top of the Ad results is important for almost all business types and it's hard to achieve that if you have low click-through rates (CTR) and poor quality scores.

If you're setting up the campaign for another business or client, make sure you send them a template to fill out. After collecting the information make sure you clarify all points before setting up the campaign.

**Summary**

We've looked at the key features to consider when setting up your campaign. Your account has been set up and you've added your billing details. You have added the voucher code and with that, you'll get free advertising credit when your account meets the terms of the voucher.

Armed with this information you can now look at setting up the campaign that will house your Ads and keywords.

# CHAPTER 2

# Campaign Type - How to Choose the Initial Campaign Options - 15 minutes

## Introduction

Next, we will look at setting up your search campaign to target people looking for your products or services. We have set up the account, added billing details and applied a voucher.

In this section, we will briefly look at the different campaign types and set up the search campaign. This section should only take about 15 minutes to complete and is largely determined by the information in your campaign brief.

## Campaign setup options

When you're first setting up a campaign, you have two setup options. You can create a campaign from scratch, or you can load settings from a previous campaign:

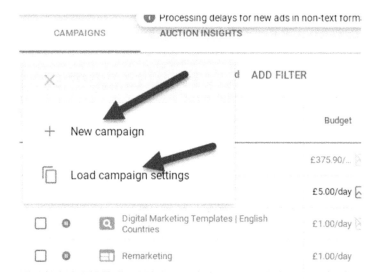

**New campaign** - because this is a brand new account with no previous campaigns, we will use this option. You will also use this option if the campaign settings are unique to this campaign and not similar to other campaigns you've created.

**Load campaign settings** - this option saves you a lot of time if you have an older campaign that will have similar settings for budget, bidding strategy, location, ad scheduling, language, and others. We will not use this option here because we are setting up our first campaign.

## Campaign goals

Your new campaign has a number of goal options to choose from. You'll select the goal option that is most relevant for your business.

Your campaign can only have one goal, so you should choose carefully. When you choose a goal, you'll see campaign suggestions to help you reach it:

**Sales** - available for Search, Display and Shopping campaign types and helps drive sales online, in-app, by phone, or in-store. This is ideal for e-commerce and online shops.

**Leads** - available for Search, Display, Shopping and Video campaign types. This is ideal if you want to get leads and other conversions by encouraging visitors to take action. Businesses that could benefit from this include local services, professional services, and any business looking to get enquiries, leads, and bookings.

**Website traffic** - available for Search, Display, Shopping and Video campaign types. Ideal if you'd like to get the right people visiting your website and in sufficient quantities.

**Product and brand consideration** - available for Display and Video campaign types and helps to encourage people to explore your products or services. Images and video are powerful tools for branding and this campaign type helps with that.

**Brand awareness and reach** - available for Display and Video campaign types. This helps you reach a broad awareness and build brand awareness and is ideal if you're an online retailer, e-commerce brand, or any business type that's looking to boost awareness.

**App promotion** - available for Universal App campaigns only. Use this to promote your app and get more installations and interactions on your app. If you have both an Android and iOS app, you can set up a campaign for each of them.

**Create a campaign without a goal's guidance** - this is available for all 5 campaign types. This gives you more flexibility in the features to use and is the right option if you want to learn more and test the features.

**Note**: the illustrations in this book will be for creating a campaign 'without a goal's guidance'.

**Example:** *Adam runs a local service business and would like to explore Google Ads. He wants to acquire leads for his new business but is not sure which campaign goal to choose. He reads the various goal types and decides to choose 'leads' because that is what he wants for his business. This option allows him to set up a Search Only campaign that targets local customers searching for his services.*

## Campaign types

The campaign type you choose determines where your ads are placed and who sees them.

Here, we will be setting up a search campaign to target people searching for your products or services. However, we will briefly look at the other campaigns so you are aware of them for future plans.

**Search** - this campaign type primarily targets people who are interested in your product or service with text ads or call ads. So your ads will appear on Google.com and Google's Search Partners. So, if you run a 'weight supplements' business and sell products online, you can bid on keywords related to the supplements you sell.

**Display** - Display Ads or image ads run on the Google Display Network (GDN). This allows you to run different types of visually appealing ads across the web on Display Partner sites, YouTube and Mobile Apps. This campaign type is great if you want to raise awareness and get new customers. So, if you're an online retailer of women's clothing, for example, you can target your audience as they visit related websites. It's not the best channel if you run an emergency service that people will normally search for.

**Shopping** - this campaign type allows you to promote your products with shopping ads. These are also known as Product Listing Ads (PLAs) and show your product's title, description, image and price. These are visually appealing and achieve a high conversion rate because people who view shopping ads are usually at the later stages of the buying funnel. This campaign type is ideal for online shops and e-commerce sites that sell products online and in-store.

**Video** - you set up a video campaign to target people on YouTube and video partner sites. You will need to link your YouTube account to your Google Ads account and set up the campaign in Google Ads. And you can run in-stream and discovery ads in the ad groups you create.

**Universal App** - this campaign type is for promoting an app to get more installs and interactions. It's an automated campaign type, so there is no keyword bidding or optimisation. Your campaign will drive app installs on the Google Search Network, Display Network, Google Play, within other apps, and on YouTube. The two mobile app platforms are Android and iOS.

**Summary**

In this chapter, we've covered the initial steps of setting up a search campaign. We've also looked briefly at the different campaign types and in what context you would use them.

We covered setting up goals for your campaign and how the Google Ads system updates its features based on the goal you choose.

# CHAPTER 3

# General Campaign Settings - 15 minutes

## Introduction

N ow we move on to general campaign settings. Here we focus on naming your campaign and why naming it correctly is important. Depending on who is managing your account you'll want to make it is easy for them to understand what each campaign is focused on.

You also get to choose the network types to advertise on. Google has three networks: Google Search Network, Google Display Network, and the YouTube Network. Your choice of campaign type determines which network will show your ads.

Finally, we will look at other campaign settings that you can update according to your campaign requirements.

## Campaign naming

Naming campaigns is one task that is fraught with errors. Many advertisers are not sure what to name their campaigns and this has a number of problems:

1. It's difficult to know what the campaign is about from the name

2. Anyone taking over the campaign struggles to understand the structuring

3. It takes up more time trying to understand what each campaign contains

Some naming mistakes I see regularly include:

1. Campaign with the same name as the business. The name of the business is obvious to anyone who will have access to your account, so don't name it after your business name.

2. Using the default name that is supplied when the campaigns are first created - like Campaign #1, Campaign #2, etc.

3. Coded titles that only the creator of the campaign understands. An example would be something like this 'PE-6755778-DC - RES'

However, you can name your campaign anything you like as long as it makes sense to you. As the owner of the account, you have the final say on the structure of your account and its features. But, if someone else will have the responsibility of managing it, you should make it easier for them and it could save you time and money.

Some ideas on how to name your campaigns are:

1. According to the products or services you offer

2. Follow the structure of your website and name campaigns according to categories

3. According to the brands you're promoting if you have multiple ones

4. Name them according to the locations you're targeting

5. According to the match types you are using (not the best though for a number of reasons)

## Choose network type

When you set up your search campaign, you have two network types to choose from:

Search Network

Display Network

These are the two main networks in Google Ads - the Search Network and the Display Network. The third one is the YouTube Network.

## The Search Network:

The Search Network includes Google.com and hundreds of partner sites known as Search partners. Your ads will appear near Google search results and other Google sites when people search for terms that are relevant to your keywords.

The 'Search Partners' helps you reach your market on other search sites that have partnered with Google. Some of these include Google-owned properties such as YouTube and hundreds of other smaller ones that provide search results.

You will want to advertise on these sites if you want to:

- Increase traffic volumes when you need more than just Google.com traffic

- Increase visitors and conversions for your products or services

- Test this traffic to assess its effectiveness

Search Partners is selected by default when you set up your campaign. And you can deselect it if it's not relevant for you.

The one drawback of advertising on search partner sites is that you don't get to see where your ads actually appeared. So there isn't a report that shows you the specific search partner websites where you got traffic from.

This means you can't optimise your ads for each partner site and you can't pick and choose where to advertise. It's either you turn them all on or all off. It's inevitable that some search partners will perform better than others and hopefully, this is a function the Google Ads team will introduce in the future.

**Example:** *Eve runs a face painting business for kids' parties. If she chooses to add the keyword 'kids face painting' in a campaign that targets search partners too, her ad will be eligible to show on Google.com and on the other hundred plus sites that make up the Search Network.*

## The Display Network

A Search Network campaign with Display Expansion increases your reach with no additional setup required and can help you reach the right audience at the right time.

To expand your reach even further, you can create a responsive ad to appear on the Display Network. Responsive ads adjust their size, appearance, and format to fit any available ad space on the Display Network.

As a new advertiser, I would advise that you leave out the Display Network at this time. First, start with Google and the Search partners and aim to get targeted ads for the search queries that will be appearing and aim for a good ROI.

You can then later add the Display Network when you are looking to increase traffic and conversions and have created some effective responsive display ads.

The Display Network includes Google sites and millions of websites, videos, and apps across the Internet that have partnered with Google. These platforms are part of the Google Adsense program and provide ad results for advertisers on third party websites.

So you can expand your reach by showing your ads on websites, videos and apps that your target audiences will be using. However, when you set up a search campaign and opt into the Display Network, your reach is limited compared to a full Display Network campaign type. That's because you aren't able to choose the websites, videos, and apps to advertise on.

Instead, the Google Ads system only shows your ads when they are predicted to be effective. Also, your ads will only run on display platforms if you aren't using all your budget on Search.

With both these networks, you can see how your ads have performed by looking at your campaign reports. You can see this at the campaign level and at the bottom of the data table you can see the 'Search' metrics and the 'Display' metrics'.

| | | | | |
|---|---|---|---|---|
| Total: Account ⑦ | £5.00/day | – | 951,364 | 10,198 Clicks |
| Total: Search campaigns ⑦ | | – | 237,222 | 6,791 Clicks |
| Total: Display campaigns ⑦ | | – | 714,142 | 3,407 Clicks |
| Total: Video campaigns ⑦ | | – | 0 | 0 |

## More general settings

These are more advanced features that you are unlikely to change when setting up a new campaign.

**Start and end dates:** the default start date is the date you set up the campaign. You can change this to any date you like and the ads will automatically start running on that date. You can also set an end date or allow the ads to run indefinitely by leaving the default settings as they are.

**Campaign URL options:** this is an advanced feature for third party tracking using a tracking template.

**Dynamic Search Ads:** this setting is for advertisers that want the Google Ads system to automate their search targeting and customise ad headlines based on their website. This has many benefits, including:

- Ability to target people who are looking for what you offer

- Ideal for advertisers with a well-developed website or a large inventory

- Filling in the gaps in your keyword campaigns by finding other relevant keywords

- Saving you a lot of time doing things like keyword research and ad text writing

**Summary**

We've looked at the different network types to choose from. Your choice of network determines a lot of factors including CTRs, conversion rates, sales, and other metrics. So, you should choose carefully during setup.

However, it's good to test some networks to see what ROI you get. You can always easily add or remove a network based on its success.

We've also covered campaign naming, the options open to you and how they affect the management of your account.

Finally, we covered additional general settings which are optional when you set up your campaign. However, updating them now or later will help make your ads more effective.

# CHAPTER 4

# Targeting & Audiences - 30 minutes

## Introduction

Targeting is one of the most important areas of Google Ads advertising. With the correct targeting, you will have done half the job of setting up an effective campaign.

Most search campaigns fail for one of the following reasons:

1. Targeting the wrong audiences

2. Insufficient budget

3. Irrelevant search terms

So, it's a must that you think through who you want to reach based on their demographics and locations. And if you're setting up a campaign for a client, you should request a brief to fully understand the audiences and set up the correct features.

For example, your campaign may be targeting a specific city or country, but because location options are not targeted correctly, your ads may reach people outside that location.

In this chapter we will be looking at some of the pitfalls to avoid and how you can set up your targeting effectively.

## Location Targeting

Location Targeting allows you to advertise to people based on where they are. So, if you want to sell widgets to people in Paris only, then make sure you are targeting Paris only and not all of France.

One way to structure your campaigns is according to the locations you're targeting. So, if you want to reach customers in 4-5 countries or cities, you can have a campaign for each of these.

Adding multiple locations in a single campaign is usually not a good idea. For example, if you are targeting the USA and the UK in the same campaign but have different shipping rates, then this can confuse people who see your ads. So, if you have features and benefits unique to each location, you should have separate campaigns for each of them.

To add a location, type it in the search box and choose the correct option from the results that appear by clicking 'Target' next to it. Be careful you pick the correct one. For example, if you are looking to target Birmingham in England, UK, make sure you don't target Birmingham in Alabama, USA.

These are the location targeting options available in your Google Ads campaign:

**Country** - one of the popular targeting options. If your product is relevant to one or more countries you can add them here. Country is also the default location option when you set up your campaign and this will show the country selection when the account was created.

**City/town** - this is the next popular option for advertisers. Here you are targeting local customers and this is a good option for local businesses such as tradesmen, accountants, restaurants, shops, and similar establishments.

**Postal code** - you can add one or multiple postal codes to target. This is highly localised and can often reach a few people. However, because of its precise nature, you will often find that conversion rates are better than other options.

**Regions** - this option allows you to target large areas within a country such as counties and states.

**Radius** - this is an advanced targeting option and is primarily for targeting a local audience. For example, a dog training business can set a radius of 10 miles from its postal address. This means it only wants to target people within a 10-mile radius.

However, from experience, radius targeting is not as accurate as other location options. It's common to receive enquiries from people who are miles away from the targeted location.

There are three main options to 'Select locations to target':

1. All countries and territories

2. United Kingdom (or the country that was selected when the account was created)

3. Enter another location

**Targeting and audiences**
Choose who you want to reach

Locations

Select locations to target ⑦

○ All countries and territories

◉ United Kingdom

○ Enter another location

∧ Location options

The default option is the country you chose when you first set up your account, which in this case is the United Kingdom. You will find that in subsequent campaigns you create the default will likely be the location you have chosen for older campaigns. This saves you a lot of time.

You can set up further campaigns quicker by just loading settings from other campaigns so you don't have to add them manually. This will save you a lot of time and ensure accuracy and consistency.

As mentioned earlier, targeting many countries and territories is usually not a good idea. Rarely should you use the 'all countries and territories' option unless you are selling a standardised product or service like a downloadable product.

The default option is to target a country, like the UK. However, if you offer a local service then this is not a good choice. The next option 'enter another location' would be more suitable.

**Enter another location**

You also have the option to 'enter a location to target or exclude'.

You can add as many countries, cities, regions, or postcodes you like that are relevant to your business. This is a search tool, and any location you enter is searched for and a number of results appear.

For example, a search for 'New York' will bring up close 'Matches' like:

New York, United States state

New York, New York, United States city

New York County, New York, United States county

Next to each of these you have the option to either 'target' 'exclude' or add 'nearby' locations to add as well, such as Pennsylvania, New Jersey, and others.

Next to each location you will see the 'reach' column that shows an estimate of how many people are in, or interested in, the location you select. This is based on the number of signed-in users visiting Google sites. New York State, for example, has a reach of 34,100,000 - one of the highest you will find online.

| Matches | Reach ⑦ | | | |
|---|---|---|---|---|
| New York, United States state | 34,000,000 | TARGET | EXCLUDE | NEARB |
| New York, New York, United States city | 27,300,000 | | | |
| New York, NY, United States Nielsen® DMA® regions | 38,500,000 | | | |
| New York County, New York, United States county | 25,000,000 | | | |
| Syracuse NY, New York, United States Nielsen® DMA® regions | 1,610,000 | | | |
| Rochester NY, New York, United States Nielsen® DMA® regions | 1,350,000 | | | |
| Utica NY, New York, United States Nielsen® DMA® regions | 388,000 | | | |
| Locations that include: New York, United States | | | | |
| United States country | 276,000,000 | | | |
| Related locations | | | | |
| Greenwich Village, New York, United States neighbourhood<br>⚑ Limited reach ⑦ | — | | | |
| 10458, New York, United States postcode | 327,000 | | | |

However, bear in mind that your actual reach is determined by the keywords you are targeting and the search queries that result from that. So, '34,100,000' is your potential market in New York, but the actual market is the people who are actually searching in that location.

You can also be more specific with your targeting. One way to do that is by targeting postcodes if you are a local service business, for example. Targeting by postcodes allows you to reach people within that postcode and write ads tailored to their needs.

## Advanced search

Advanced Search is a location feature that gives you more flexibility with your targeting. You can add a lot more locations in bulk and you can use radius targeting to reach people within a certain radius.

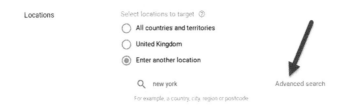

## Bulk locations

Google Ads allows you to add up to 1,000 locations in your campaign. You do that by selecting the 'add locations in bulk' button and then list them vertically in the box - one location per line. You can paste or type them with each location on a separate line.

◉ Location  ○ Radius

☑ Add locations in bulk

Locations can be cities, postcodes, countries, etc. Enter one location per line.

0 / 1000

Restrict locations within a country (optional)          SEARCH

Your locations can be countries, cities, towns, postcodes, and so on, and you can add up to 1,000 rather than adding each location one by one, which can be time-consuming.

If you want to target more than 1,000 locations, you can add them in bulk multiple times. So, you can start by adding 1,000 locations and when you've finished, add another 200, to have a total of 1,200 locations.

If you are targeting a city, make sure you include the country or state it is in, for example, Portsmouth, England, and that goes for postcodes too, like 94103, California.

Remember to click 'save' when you are done, or you could lose all the locations you have added.

Any location that is not recognised by Google will not be added. Google only permits targeting for locations that adhere to minimum privacy thresholds where minimum area and minimum user counts are met. So you will find many neighbourhoods and locales cannot be added as locations, because they don't meet the minimum user count.

## Radius targeting

Radius targeting is an advanced targeting feature. It allows you to enter a place name, address, or coordinates, and target people within a specified radius of that location. So you can add a postcode and then target people within a 5-mile radius or 10-km radius, for example.

This targeting option is useful for businesses that want to target local customers that fall within the vicinity of the business. For example, a plumber who can only travel as far as 20 miles from their address would find radius targeting the best targeting option.

It's worth bearing in mind that when you target a small radius that could mean your ads only show intermittently or none at all. That's because small targets might not meet Google's targeting criteria.

One disadvantage of using radius targeting is that it is not uncommon to receive enquiries and leads from outside of the radius. This is likely due to IP address allocation by ISPs, and so people outside of the area may have the same IPs as people in the targeted area.

To get started with radius targeting, follow these steps:

1. Click the 'Advanced search' link

2. Select the 'Radius' button

3. Enter a place name, address, or coordinates in the box and choose the miles or kilometres you want to target. For example, a 10-mile radius around the postcode MK5

4. The system will then do a quick search and bring up the specific location you want to target and will show at least 3 or 4 other relevant ones you can choose instead. Select the relevant one by clicking the 'Target' link

5. In the map to the right of your screen, you will be able to see the area that the radius covers. If everything looks good, then click the 'Save' button.

6. You can add multiple locations that are relevant to your campaign

## Advanced Location Options

This is one of the most consuming features in the settings section and for good reason. Many advertisers ignore it altogether and this can prove costly over an extended period.

It usually comes as a big surprise to many advertisers when they look at their geographic reports and user location reports to find they have been getting clicks from people outside their targeted locations. And this is despite the fact they have added specific locations to target and have excluded all the locations they don't want to appear in.

When they've added more locations to exclude from their geographic and user location reports, they still find they continue to appear in other undesirable areas. All the while this is wasting their budget and time.

Location options is an advanced feature that lets you 'Target' or 'Exclude' people based on where they are likely to be located and the places they've shown interest in.

^ Location options

Target ⑦
⦿ People in, or who show interest in, your targeted locations (recommended)
○ People in or regularly in your targeted locations
○ People searching for your targeted locations

Exclude ⑦
⦿ People in your excluded locations (recommended)
○ People in, or who show interest in, your excluded locations

The 'Target' section provides you with three targeting options:

- People in, or who show interest in, your targeted locations (recommended)

- People in or regularly in your targeted locations

- People searching for your targeted locations.

By default, your campaign will be set to target 'people in, or who show interest in', your targeted locations. This is also the option Google recommends for most advertisers.

However, the problem here is your ads will be eligible to thousands or millions of people who are interested but may not be serviceable for your business. For example, if you sell widgets online and sell only to the UK, people in France who want to purchase widgets from the UK will see your ads and click. And this will be wasted budget spend.

However, it's important to know that people who are not actually in your targeted location may prove to be a good market to target. For example, a photographer based in Glasgow will likely be interested in people who are in London that are actually looking for a photographer based in Glasgow.

Similarly, hotels often target people that are thousands of miles from their location. But often the best way to do this is to create specific campaigns for those locations and create ads tailored to them.

This can be time-consuming of course, especially if there are many locations to target, but it can be worth it if you want to achieve high click-through rates (CTR) and quality scores.

It's important to remember that advanced location options only apply to ads on the Search and Display Networks.

## People in or regularly in your targeted locations:

This is the ideal setting for most businesses, especially local service businesses or businesses that deliver only in the targeted location. It helps you target people who are likely to be located, or who are regularly located in, your target area.

So this doesn't include people who search for your targeted locations but whose physical location was outside the target location at the time of searching.

The Google Ads system uses a number of signals to determine where someone's physical location is and whether to show your ad. Someone's computer or mobile device helps to determine their physical location and these factors are taken into consideration:

- **IP address:** a searcher's location is usually based on the Internet Protocol (IP) address, which is a unique number assigned to each computer by Internet Service Providers. If the searcher's device is connected to a Wi-Fi Network, the Ads system may detect the Wi-Fi network's IP address to determine physical location.

- **Device location:** the location settings on a user's device may be able to help the Google Ads system use a precise location for advertising, based on GPS, Wi-Fi, and Bluetooth settings.

**People searching for your targeted locations:**

A third option in the 'Target' section is to target people who are searching for your targeted locations. So, if a person includes a location you are targeting in their keyword search then your ad will show for them. However, if they don't specify a location in their search then the Google Ads system uses their physical location for targeting.

*Example:* *John runs a business in a French ski resort that provides chalets to families and couples. He wants to target people in the United Kingdom who want to book a holiday in the ski resort. So, he creates a search campaign targeting the UK and sets language targeting to English. He also updates advanced location options to target 'people in or regularly in your targeted locations'.*

## Excluded locations

You can also choose to exclude certain locations from seeing your ad. For example, if you are targeting London, you can exclude particular postcodes from that city.

The 'Exclude' section provides you with two options:

- People in your excluded locations (recommended)

- People in, or who show interest in, your excluded locations

The default setting is to exclude 'people in your excluded locations'. So, any excluded locations that you add in the location targeting section will be blocked.

However, you should be aware that people who show interest in your excluded locations may still be able to see and click your ads. So, you may want to change it to exclude 'people in, or who show interest in, your excluded locations' if you don't want these people seeing your ad.

***Example***: *Enoch runs a B&B in Cornwall and has set up two campaigns with two Location types: campaign 1 targets people in Cornwall and campaign 2 targets everyone outside* of Cornwall who's interested in a B&B in Cornwall. So in campaign 2, she sets her targeted location option to target only 'people searching for your targeted locations'. This helps her control the messages for both campaigns and keep them relevant.

## Languages

Like location targeting, you can add one language or multiple languages to target. However, with language targeting, it's strongly advised to have one language to target.

For example, to show ads to people with French as a language preference, select French as your campaign language and use French Ad text and keywords.

You should select the languages your customers speak and your ads will show to customers with these language preferences, or on sites with these languages. Bear in mind that Google doesn't translate ads or keywords.

On the Search Network, your campaign can target one language, multiple languages or all languages. At times you may find it helpful to target multiple languages because by doing so you can reach people who speak more than one language and may search in several languages.

Google uses a number of signals to understand the language the user knows, and it attempts to service the best ad available in a language the person understands. These signals include the search language, the user's settings and other signals as derived by machine learning algorithms.

To get started, click the search box to add the languages you want to target.

A box will open with a list of all languages that can be targeted in Google Ads. There are about 48 in total you can target and you can select the most relevant for your campaign.

You also have the option to target 'All languages' but as mentioned earlier this is usually not a good idea - especially if your audiences speak specific languages. Finally, click the 'Save' button.

**Example:** *Jane understands both English and Spanish and while her desktop browser is set to a Spanish interface, her other activity on Google strongly suggests she speaks English too. Many of her search queries are also in English such as 'buy dress online' so she would be eligible to see ads that target either English or Spanish when the keywords match.*

## Display Network language targeting

On the Display Network, people aren't searching for your products or services, but they are browsing third party websites and apps. However, language targeting works similarly here too as Google looks at the language of the website or app someone is viewing or has recently viewed to determine which ads to show. So the Google Ads system looks at either pages or apps the user has seen or the page they're currently viewing.

**Example:** *John has been viewing several blogs related to technology on the Google Display Network that are written in Chinese and sees ads targeted at Chinese speakers. Later, he may still see Chinese Ads on other blogs in the Display Network that are written in English because of his viewing history.*

## Audiences

Audiences is the third and last targeting option in your new campaign. You can either set this up now or wait until later when you have sufficient data to set up good audience lists.

According to Google, audiences are 'groups of people with specific interests, intents and demographics...that you can show your ads to.'

The data from your audiences may be used to improve the bidding and targeting of your audience campaigns.

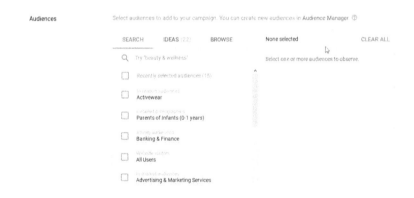

**Note**: For your new campaign, audiences may not be important at this stage, but will come in handy later when you have more data and want to target more precisely. However, a brief understanding of each of them is helpful at this stage.

The focus of the campaign is to target people who are searching based on their intent - regardless of their demographics - and that will be discussed in chapter 11.

The three main audiences available to you are:

**Demographics (who they are)**

This targets people in your target market based on their parental status, marital status, education, and homeownership status.

**In-market (what they're actively researching or planning)**

This is about reaching people as they are actively researching or planning for things such as baby products, apparel, clothing, business services, dating services, employment services, software, and much more.

**Remarketing and similar audiences (how they've interacted with your business)**

This option allows you to reach out to people who have visited your website before. There are two main list types you can target: website visitors and similar audiences.

Website visitors are the audiences you've created and you can retarget in your search campaign and similar audiences are audiences that closely match the visitors who have been on your site before.

**Summary**

We've covered the main targeting features you need to set before advertising. These settings including location, language, and audiences, which determine who do and don't see your ads.

As mentioned in the opening of this chapter, targeting is one of the important factors you need to get right from the beginning. Of course, some of your successes will come from testing, but you should be sure of who you want to target before starting.

Some features you'll update as you manage your campaign and see its performance. Next, we look at budgets and bidding, which help you to reach the audiences you want to target.

# CHAPTER 5

# Budgets & Bidding - 15 minutes

## Introduction

Budgets and bidding are two areas fraught with errors in Google Ads. This is mainly the case during setup because you have little information to go on and have to test different budgets and bid strategies.

The main challenge is that there are many options to choose from and that can be confusing for a new advertiser.

However, if you're prepared and willing to do some testing, with a little patience, you can achieve the best settings for your campaign. Fortunately, Google Ads offers many testing options and you can run tests for as long as you want and spend as little or as much as you like.

In this chapter, we will look at all the features in budgets and bidding and I'll offer recommendations for your new campaign to get you quickly started.

## Budget setting

In October 2017, Google (source: support.google.com) announced that campaigns would now be able to spend up to twice the average daily budget. According to Google, this is to 'help you reach your advertising goals, like clicks and conversions'.

So, don't be surprised to find that if you have a £20 daily budget, for example, to see your spend go up to £40 on some days. What Google promises, however, is that you will not be charged more than your monthly charging limit: that is, the average number of days in a month (30.4) multiplied by your average daily budget.

It's also important to note that this spending is balanced by the days when your spend is below your daily budget. However, where you pay for conversions, your daily spend will at times exceed your average daily budget by more than twice.

Budget setting is one of those challenges that every new advertiser faces. And established advertisers also struggle to find the right budget for each of their campaigns.

Of course, every advertiser wants to pay as little as possible to achieve their goals. But that often leads to missed opportunities, which affects the overall performance of the campaign.

For example, some search types are 'transactional' in nature and are therefore valuable for all advertisers. This means there will usually be many competitors looking to bid on the same keywords, and so having a low budget means your site is unlikely to appear for them at auction time - and instead appear for informational searches, which are unlikely to convert.

So, the budget you set should be sufficient to help you reach your advertising goals.

Budget        Enter the average you want to spend each day

£

Here are some budget setting options to help you decide:

1. Set a test budget - this is often the best option when starting. Many advertisers start with a budget between $300 and $600 in the first month to test the waters.

2. Keyword research – use the keyword research tool to find out the potential traffic you could get with the keywords you choose, and then set a budget (we will cover this later when setting up ad groups).

## Bidding

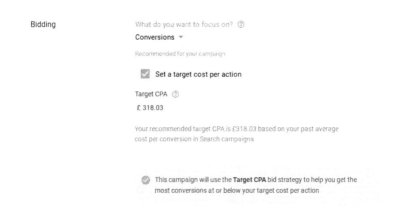

There are two main bidding strategy types: automated and manual bidding. With automated bidding, the Google Ads system sets bids automatically and does all the heavy lifting for you. It essentially sets the bids and determines your ad position in the auction result.

With manual bidding, bid setting is up to you. You decide what bids to set for your campaigns, ad groups, and keywords based on goals. Bear in mind that this can be time-consuming and should be avoided if you have little time or experience.

**Automated bidding strategies:**

**Target Cost Per Acquisition (CPA)**

This is one of the four smart bidding strategies that help you bid for conversions and conversion value. The other three are Target ROAS, Maximise Conversions, and Enhanced CPC, which are listed below.

Target CPA aims to help you get as many conversions as possible for your budget. The system will decide on the bids and set them according to your targeted acquisition cost.

However, some conversions will cost more and some less, but it will aim to get as close to your target as possible. The Google Ads system will provide a recommended target CPA and you can choose to accept or reject it.

You are unlikely to use this bid strategy at the beginning. That's because you need to have some historic conversion data to calculate the recommended CPA target.

## Target ROAS

This is one of the more complicated bidding strategies. This is the average conversion value (expressed as a percentage) that you'd like to get for every dollar you spend. Google Ads automatically sets bids to get you as much conversion value as possible at a targeted return on ad spend (ROAS). It will recommend target ROAS and you can choose to accept it or set your own. However, if you set it too low that could affect conversions and bidding and the campaign could underperform.

Bidding

Back to previous bidding options

Select your bid strategy ⑦
Target ROAS

Target ROAS ⑦
59.338 %

Your recommended target ROAS is 59%

Use a portfolio strategy

If your goal, for example, is to get an average $5 in sales for every $1 you spend, your target ROAS would be 500%.

The formula to work this out is:

Target ROAS = Conversion value divided by ad spend X 100%

## Maximise Conversions

Your bids are set automatically to help your campaign get the most conversions possible for your budget. Choosing this option means ads and keywords with the best performance will receive more exposure.

Bidding       Back to previous bidding options

Select your bid strategy ⑦

Maximise conversions      ▼

Use a portfolio strategy

## Maximise Clicks

Use an automated strategy like Maximise Clicks when you launch a campaign for the first time. That's because you are unlikely to know what bids to set for your ads and so you should allow Google Ads to set the bids automatically. However, some people report that Google bids too high with this bid strategy, so you should consider placing a maximum bid limit at the campaign level.

## Enhanced CPC

Google adjusts your manual bids to get you the most conversions. You can use this bid strategy with a Manual CPC strategy and it will increase bids by up to 30% for good keywords and reduce it by up to 100% for poor keywords.

## Target Impression Share

In 2019 Google removed the competitor bidding strategy 'Target Outranking Share' and replaced it with the 'Target Impression Share' bidding strategy. Target Outranking Share was quite effective at helping advertisers outrank specific competitors, but not necessarily all of them.

However, Target Impression Share has proven quite effective too and is worth checking out when you want to achieve higher ad rankings.

Target Impression Share is a smart bidding strategy. It is an automated bid strategy that sets bids with the goal of getting your ads to the absolute top of the page (typically before you see organic search results), or anywhere on the first page of Google search results.

It is only available for the Google Search Network (including Search Partners) and helps you achieve your Impression Share goal in your campaign.

## Absolute top of results page

Unlike Target Outranking Share bidding strategy, this strategy has more advantages, including helping you to outrank all competitors. So, instead of picking one specific competitor to outrank, you can choose to outrank all competitors by choosing the 'Absolute top of results page' option.

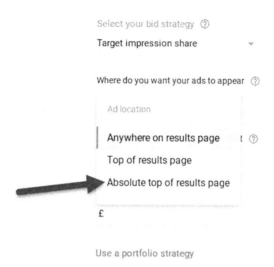

This will place your ad in the first position at the top of the first page of search results. You will also set what percentage of the impression share you want to target in this position and it can be anything from 1% to 100%.

The 'Percent (%) Impression Share to target' is how often you want your ads to appear in the search page area you select when other people search for your keywords.

Next, you must set a 'Maximum CPC bid limit' to prevent your costs spiralling out of control. The maximum CPC limit is the maximum amount you are willing to pay for each click. You will usually pay much less than this, but be aware that if your maximum bid does not meet the bid for your ad to appear on the first page of results you may see lower conversions.

**Example:** *James runs ads for an accountancy practice targeting small local businesses in his area. He consistently finds that his ad positions are lower than his competitors' and is missing out on many keyword opportunities because of low rank and low click-through rate. James then decides to change from a Manual CPC bid strategy to a Target Impression Share bid strategy and chooses the option to appear at the absolute top of the results page with a £5 bid limit.*

## Anywhere on results page

This option places your ad anywhere on the first page of search results. So that can be at the top of the page, above the organic search results, or below the page under the organic results.

You are likely to pay less for the clicks that you receive and therefore spend less on the campaign. However, lower positions can also affect conversion rates and overall performance.

Set a 'Percent (%) Impression Share to target' to determine how often you want your ads to appear anywhere on the results page when other people search for your keywords.

And put a 'Maximum CPC bid limit' to cap the amount you want to pay for each click.

**Top of results page**

With the 'Top of results page' option, you're looking to get your ad to the top of the page among one of the top 4 ads.

Like the two options mentioned above, you will set a 'Percent (%) Impression share to target' and set a maximum CPC bid limit.

**Bidding strategies**

When to use Automated Bidding:

1. When you first launch your ads

2. When bidding for conversions and conversion value

3. When looking to outbid a competitor like the Target Outranking Share Bid Strategy

## Manual CPC

Manual CPC is the only manual bidding strategy in Google Ads. It has far fewer options to choose from than the automated bid strategies we've talked about above. Basically with Manual CPC, you get to set the maximum amount you would like to pay for each click.

When To Use Manual Bidding:

1. When you want to control bidding yourself

2. When you want to launch a campaign if you are sure what bids to set

However, manual CPC bidding can be time-consuming and result in lower performance if not done right. It can limit your campaign from reaching its full potential.

There is an option to combine your manual bidding with automated bidding. Enhanced cost per click is an automated bid strategy that helps you get more conversions from manual bidding. It works by raising your bids for clicks that are likely to lead to conversions and lowering them for those that seem less likely to convert.

To use this option, select Enhanced CPC in the Manual CPC bid strategy, as the image shows below:

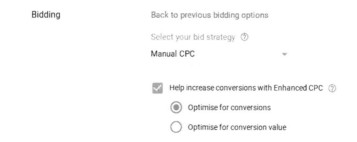

## Ad scheduling

Ad scheduling or 'day parting' as it is sometimes known, allows you to set the days and hours to run your ads. The default setting is to allow ads to run on all days and for all hours.

Clearly, this doesn't work for every business. If, for example, you're targeting B2B customers, you would likely benefit from running your ads from Monday to Friday during working hours. However, it can be argued that if people are searching at all times including weekends and evenings, then you should target them at those times too.

Many business owners work on weekends and evenings and they happen to be the only decision-makers in their businesses. These could all be valuable customers to target and you may never reach them if you run ads only during working hours.

When launching a new campaign, it's often best to run ads 24/7. Your time reports will then show which your best days and hours are for clicks and conversions.

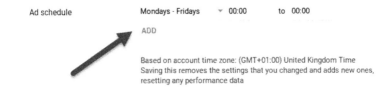

Ad schedule      Mondays - Fridays    ▾   00:00     to   00:00

ADD

Based on account time zone: (GMT+01:00) United Kingdom Time
Saving this removes the settings that you changed and adds new ones, resetting any performance data

## Ad rotation

In each ad group you create, you should have between 3 to 5 ads for testing purposes. These ads should be rotated and shown to visitors based on settings you assign in the Ad Rotation feature.

You can either allow Google Ads to decide which ads to show based on their performance or you can decide yourself.

There are two main options to help you decide which ad in each ad group is shown for a search query:

- Optimize: Prefer best performing ads

- Do not optimize: Rotate ads indefinitely

Ad rotation

- ● Optimise: Prefer best performing ads
- ○ Do not optimise: Rotate ads indefinitely
- ○ Optimise for conversions (Not supported)
- ○ Rotate evenly (Not supported)

## Optimize: Prefer best performing ads

This is the default option when you first set up your campaign. It's the option Google recommends for most advertisers. The system rotates your ads and shows those ads that are expected to receive more clicks or conversions.

## Do not optimize: Rotate ads indefinitely

For more experienced users who want to run split or A/B tests, this may be a better option. Google Ads will show ads more evenly for an indefinite amount of time.

This means that low performing ads will run about as often as your best-performing ads for an indefinite period - which could be bad if not done right.

This option is not recommended for most advertisers because it requires testing experience and also involves a lot of work. If you don't test effectively, your poor performing ads will run equally alongside the good ones and this will affect click and conversion performance.

**Summary**

We've looked at budgets and bidding: two features you should set up now as you work on your campaign and you'll update as you manage it.

We have also covered ad scheduling and ad rotation - two features that may not need updating at this time during launch. Instead, as you assess campaign performance, you can update these in line with results.

Try not to overthink this part of the setup. Your goal as always when setting up a campaign is to test the different features and you can do that with a limited budget and adjust accordingly.

The performance of your campaigns will greatly inform future changes you make. It will also help you launch future campaigns more effectively.

# CHAPTER 6

# Ad Extensions - 25 minutes

## Introduction

Over the years, Google has added new features to help enhance text ads. This is to make ads relevant to searchers and to increase click-through rates, conversions and overall performance.

These improvements have also been designed to prevent people who are not relevant to your business from clicking ads.

Previously, text ads only had one headline, a short description and a final URL. This was the norm. You can now see up to 8 lines of text with a phone number and location details for top-ranked ads.

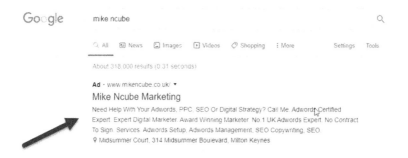

These additions are known as ad extensions and they help improve your ad performance. With ad extensions, you will see greater prominence in ad results and this leads to more clicks and conversions.

## What are ad extensions?

Ad extensions are features that appear below the main part of your ad:

As you can see, the main part of the ad includes two headlines, a description and a URL. We will cover the structure of an ad in chapter 7 when we create your text ads.

Adding ad extensions means you have more prominence in the search results. You also benefit from a higher click-through rate (CTR) because of greater prominence on the page.

It's okay to run your campaign without ad extensions but you will be at a serious disadvantage. This is quite common with new advertisers who have little knowledge of what ad extensions are and how they work.

However, Google has recently added them at the campaign setting level which means new advertisers are unlikely to miss them.

**Ad extensions**

Get up to 15% higher clickthrough rate by showing additional information on your ads

Sitelink extensions      Add additional links to your ad

Callout extensions      Add more business information to your ad

Call extensions      Add a phone number to your ad

⊕ Ad extension

## Sitelinks

Sitelinks are one of the most popular ad extensions. They are part of the three primary extensions, alongside callouts and call extensions.

They provide links to other pages on your website that are likely to be important to your searchers. You may not always be sure what people are actually looking for. You also might have returning visitors who may be interested in other pages on your site that they may not be aware of. Sitelinks provide more options to visitors, helping to capture them more than a link to one page on your website will.

Ad · www.mikencube.co.uk/ ▾
**Mike Ncube Marketing**
Need Help With Your Adwords, PPC, SEO Or Digital Strategy? Call Me. Expert Digital Marketer No.1 UK Adwords Expert. Award Winning Marketer. Adwords Certified Expert. No Contract To Sign. Services: Adwords Setup, Adwords Management, SEO Copywriting, SEO.

| Get In Touch | About Mike Ncube |
|---|---|
| Call Me Now To Discuss Your Adwords Needs And To Launch Your Campaigns. | I'm a Certified Adwords Expert With Over 11 Years PPC Experience. |
| Client Reviews | PPC Case Study |
| See What Past Clients Have To Say About My Adwords PPC Service. | Find Out How I IncreasedThe BIS Conversion Rate by 10% In Days. |

For example, a potential customer may be interested in FAQs, so why not present that option to them? Of course, your site's navigation should make it easy for people to reach those pages but that's not always the case.

Also, from your knowledge gleaned from past visitors, you'll know which other pages they may be interested in - so show them that option in the ad.

The one big difference between sitelinks and other ad extensions is they are clickable. This means they are the only extensions that send visitors to your website. Of course, call and message extensions are clickable too, but not in the way sitelinks are, as we will discuss below.

The structure of sitelinks is similar to the old standard text ad format. But this is not an issue because the role of sitelinks is to include punchy text. It includes:

- Sitelinks Text (headlines) - 25 characters
- Description line 1 - 35 characters
- Description line 2 - 35 characters
- Final URL

As you'll see, sitelink text is a requirement but the descriptions are only optional.

I would recommend adding the descriptions. When they appear with your main ad, they give your listing even more prominence and leads to higher click through rates.

Also, Google Ads rewards ads with sitelink descriptions with higher rankings. And it's usually only the top-ranked ad that will show the description.

Ideally, you should add 4 or more sitelinks - as many as possible. Not all of them will show at all times, as only those links most relevant to the search query and the best-performing links will show. This relates to callout extensions, too.

One thing to note is that a sitelink will not show if it has the same text as the main ad. So make sure you make them unique and have different text from the main ad and your callout extensions.

**Callouts**

Callouts are designed to 'call out' an important benefit or feature related to your product or service. These appear under your main text ad and are not clickable, unlike sitelinks.

Their main job is to highlight something important like an offer, delivery rate, benefit and so on. You need to add at least two callout extensions for them to be eligible to appear.

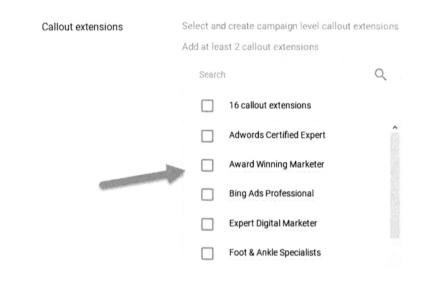

Google's advice to advertisers is to add as many as possible so that the system selects the best ones to run. Also, don't add any feature or benefit that's already mentioned in the main ad, because the callout extension will not show.

Each callout has a maximum of 25 characters of text, including spaces. That should equate to about 2 or 3 words maximum. You don't have a lot of space to play with, so creative writing is important.

However, Google has deliberately made them this short for a reason. On mobile devices, long text is usually truncated or will not appear at all, so if you want the callouts to show, try to keep the text at a minimum. If mobile is important for you, try and use as little text as possible - maybe even one word per callout if you can get away with it.

For example, don't say 'Free Delivery Available'; just say 'Free Delivery' instead. It won't lose its meaning.

## Call

A call extension aims to display your phone number to get visitors calling. This will appear next to your ad and you can add both cell phone and landline numbers.

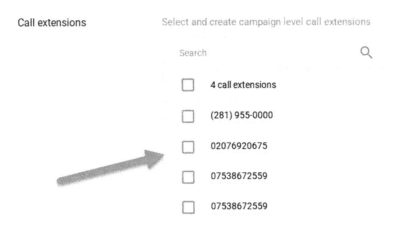

**Call extensions** — Select and create campaign level call extensions

You can also add as many numbers as you like, however, one is usually the norm and that should suffice to get calls to your business. Call extensions are most effective on mobile devices that allow people to call directly from your ad and connect straight to your business.

You can also add the option of call reporting to track people who call from your ads. That can be very powerful in helping you see which of your ads, campaigns, and keywords are working best for you.

Setting this up is relatively easy and all you need to do is select the country you're targeting, add your phone number, and select call reporting.

## Location

Location extensions are especially important for local retailers and local service businesses. They allow you to display your business address next to your ad. This is important if you'd like people to visit your business and get directions directly on their phone.

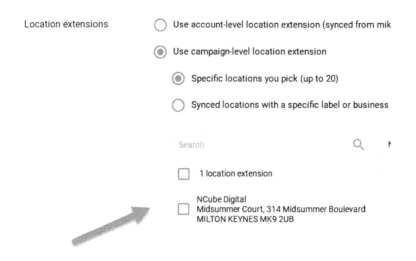

Visitors can click your extension to get further details about your location and the most relevant business information in one place. Your location extension will at times show your phone number, allowing people to call directly from their phones.

To get started with location extensions, first set up a Google My Business Account and add all your business addresses. Next, link it to your Google Ads account and select the locations you want to show in your campaigns.

**Example:** *Noah is the owner of a local cake shop and wants to increase traffic and customers to her store. So she launches a campaign and adds location extensions by linking her Google My Business account to her Google Ads account. Now, when local people search for 'cake shop near me' or 'local cake shop' her extension is eligible to show and may give cake lovers the distance to her shop, her address and a clickable 'call' button. They'll get to visit a details page which includes information like opening hours, phone number, photos of her business and cakes, and directions to the shop.*

**Message**

Some of your visitors may not want to call your business. Instead, they may want to communicate via email or text message. Message extensions make that possible.

Visitors can contact you directly via text message and email on their smartphones and desktops. Turning on message reporting means you will have tracking data to see which ads are driving enquiries.

There are a few features to set up when creating your message extensions:

1. Add the email address you use to receive messages.

2. Add the phone number where you'll receive messages.

3. Include your business name.

4. Enter extension text. This should be a call to action that gets visitors responding and allows up to 35 characters.

There is a default message you can use or customise but it should not exceed the 35 character limit.

5. I encourage you to add a default customer message that pre-populates in the visitors messaging app. This makes it easier for your visitor to make contact and increases your conversion rate. You can customise the suggestion provided but remember to keep it within the 100 character limit.

6. There's also an option to an add auto-reply message which automatically sends a message to your customers

## Price

Price extensions are one of the less used extensions. They allow you to add pricing for your products or services. Of course, you can add prices in the main ad, but this is a better option if you have multiple products or services and print structures.

You can test these to see how they perform for your ads, but it's often not a good idea to display your prices if they are likely to change or you send out quotes to potential customers.

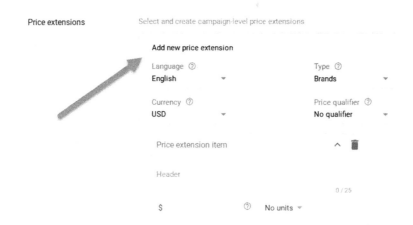

Price extensions    Select and create campaign-level price extensions

Add new price extension

Language ⑦                          Type ⑦
English            ▼                Brands            ▼

Currency ⑦                         Price qualifier ⑦
USD               ▼                No qualifier      ▼

Price extension item                        ∧  🗑

Header

                                        0 / 25

$              ⑦    No units ▼

## Promotion

Promotion extensions are a new feature and they allow you to offer a discount for occasions such as Black Friday, Boxing Day, back to school, Christmas, and so on.

You can set a start and end date for the promotion and also add a description and final URL.

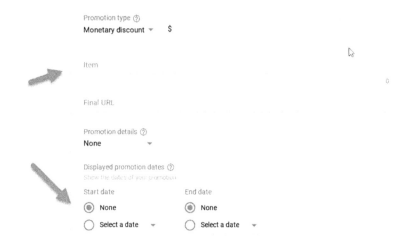

## Structured snippets

Structured snippet extensions are becoming more popular with advertisers. They are similar to callout extensions and allow you to highlight features and benefits about your products or services.

With structured snippets, you'll add a 'header' that reflects a category, service, feature or product that your business offers. Then you'll add at least three values related to the header you've added. Each value has a 25-character space limit and you can add up to 10 values.

The 'header' types available are amenities, brands, courses, degree programs, featured hotels, destinations, and a few others.

An example header for a university would be 'degree programs' and then a list of up to 10-degree programs in the 'values'.

## Summary

Setting up ad extensions is a must. Without them, your ads will underperform in all important elements, such as ad rank, ad position, CTR, conversions, and quality score.

Of course, it's not necessary to add all the different ad extension types, but at a minimum, you should have sitelinks, callouts, and call extensions. Most business types should have all three and you should add as many of each as possible.

Next, add location extensions to show your address and map directions. This is important for local businesses and retailers. You should also add structured snippet and promotion extensions when they make sense for your business.

As part of your campaign management, you'll add, update and optimise your extensions. We will cover this in Section Two where we look at managing your campaign.

Now that you've completed the account settings, you'll move on to setting up the ads, keywords, and ad groups.

# CHAPTER 7

# Ad Group Setup - 1 hour

## Introduction

This part of the campaign setup deals with the assets visible to searchers. This is the only part of your campaign searchers see and allows you to connect with them directly.

Most of what we've covered in this book so far is not visible to your targeted audience - but has a very important part to play in achieving your advertising goals.

However, with ads and keywords, you only have a few seconds or minutes to connect with your audience. Get this wrong and much of the work you've done so far won't count for much.

We will start by setting up your first ad group. This includes keyword research and writing text ads that are triggered when people search on Google.

**First ad group setup**

We will start with keyword research to find the keywords you will bid on. These should be relevant to the searches people conduct on Google and should be related to your ads.

Later, you will learn how to use the Keyword Planner tool to research and build a list of targeted keywords. For now, we will use the keyword research tool that's in your ad group.

An ad group contains one or more ads and a set of related keywords. To achieve the best result, focus all the ads and keywords in the group on one product or service. This will help you achieve high quality scores for your keywords and improve your ad performance.

To find for keywords to bid on with this new ad group, enter your website or a related website in the box and click enter:

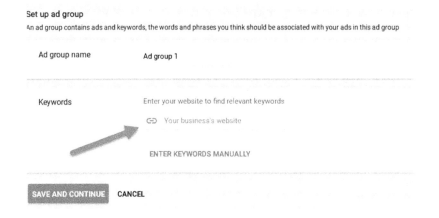

The tool will then search the website for potential keywords you can add. This is one important reason why you should have well-written content on your website. If you find it brings up keywords that are not closely related to what you sell or provide, then it means your website or landing page is not optimised.

You'll need to update your website and make sure each page is optimised with targeted keywords. This also helps with your Search Engine Optimisation (SEO), so you can rank high on Google.

As you can see, this provides a keyword list and the related monthly search volume for each keyword. The highest volume keywords appear at the top and the lowest volume at the bottom, so you can quickly see your volume drivers and long-tail keywords.

You can also add any keywords manually if there are any that come to mind. Because of your knowledge of your products or services, it shouldn't be too hard to come up with 5 good keywords to add to the list.

Set up ad group
An ad group contains ads and keywords, the words and phrases you think should be associated with your ads

Ad group name          Ad group 1

Keywords               Enter your website to find relevant keywords

                       ⊖   Your business's website

                       ENTER KEYWORDS MANUALLY

SAVE AND CONTINUE   CANCEL

Try to add between 5-15 keywords per ad group. Anything below this means you are likely to miss out on possible relevant search terms. If you add too many keywords - over 15 - you risk having keywords that are not very relevant and this can affect CTRs and quality scores.

Follow the rule of two when selecting keywords to add. This rule states that your two primary words should be in each keyword you add to the ad group.

For example, if you are a loft ladder supplier and you have an ad group for 'loft installations' the rule states that every keyword should have the words loft installations and close variants such as:

- Loft installations

- Loft hatch installation

- Loft hatch installation in Redditch

- Find loft hatch installer

These are all closely related and you can place them in the same ad group in different match types too.

Besides adding keywords, you should also add match types to control search terms. There are 4 keyword match types in Google Ads and each controls the type of searches it matches the ads to:

## Broad match

Broad match keywords target a wider range of searches than the other three match types and is the default match type. Besides targeting exact searches for your keywords, it also targets synonyms, misspellings, close variants, plurals/singulars, stemming, and other related searches.

Using our example above for 'loft installations', if you add a broad match version of it, the keyword will be added as *loft installation* with no modifications.

It's best not to launch a new campaign with broad match keywords. This is because it's unlikely you will have built a comprehensive keyword list to block any irrelevant searches. Instead, you will add these later when you have built a good negative list and are looking to target a wider range of search types and increase clicks and sales.

## Broad match modified (BMM)

BMM is similar to broad match type above, except important words in the keyword are designated with a + sign like this: +loft +installations

The purpose of the + sign is to trigger the ad *only* when the words with the + sign appear in the search term. For example:

- loft installations - will trigger the ad

- loft installation in Hull - will trigger the ad because 'loft installation' is in the query

- loft storage - will not trigger the ad because the word *installations* is not in this query

**Phrase match**

Phrase match keywords are designated with quotation marks like 'loft installations''. For your ads to trigger, the search term should have the words *loft installations* in the same order and can appear with additional words before or after. The ad will not trigger if there is a word in the middle such as *loft service installations*.

Phrase match is a good match type to start with, along with exact and broad match modified keywords. It gives you greater control over the searches you target and means your ads are unlikely to appear for unrelated searches.

## Exact match

Exact match is the most restrictive of the 4 keyword match types. That's because it only appears for exact searches and close variations of it. This includes plurals, singulars, misspellings and similar - but not synonyms.

Exact match keywords are designated with brackets like [loft installations]. The ad will appear only when the searches are exactly the same, however, it will also appear for:

- Loft installer - close variant

- Loft instalation - misspelling

- Loft installation - singular

However, Google has made some changes to exact match keywords and ads are now appearing for a limited number of synonyms. According to Google, these are highly targeted searches with similar user intent to the exact keyword.

You won't usually need to add negative keywords if you add exact match keywords only. However, exact match is very restrictive and you should add phrase and modified broad matches to your new campaign.

Now you've added between 5-15 keywords in different match types, you can now click *Save and Continue* to create your ads.

## Ad creation

Next, we will set up the ads people will see when they search for your products or services. The ad is the only part of your account besides the ad extensions that people will see.

These must be highly targeted and relate to search intent. It doesn't mean you have to be a great copywriter to write great ads, but it certainly requires some thinking to create differentiated ads that get people clicking and converting.

Here are some things to consider as you create your ads:

## Call to action

What action do you want visitors to take on your website? This should be explicit in the ad and shouldn't confuse your visitors. Use actionable phrases such as 'buy now' or 'book today'.

## Features & Benefits

A mix of features and benefits in the ad is acceptable but benefits are usually more important. You want to make it clear to visitors what they get from your products or services. Making this clear in the ad means you can select your target market quicker and anyone not interested doesn't click - this will save you a lot of money. You should also avoid deceptive or cryptic messages as these are likely to be disapproved by Google.

## Discounts & Offers

Everyone wants cheaper products and services and that holds true for your customers. So, if you have a coupon or discount offer, make sure you add it in your ad. Your offer should also be available on the landing page.

## Free stuff

One powerful way to elicit interest in your ads is to offer something free. Ads with free offers consistently perform ads without. Free shipping is a powerful example. According to Google Research, free shipping outperforms money-off discounts and coupons, leading to higher CTRs and conversions.

## Keyword

By all means, try to include your keyword in the ad, especially in the headline. People are more likely to click an ad if they see their keyword in it. If the keyword is included in the description you'll often see it in bold letters, so it stands out from the rest of the ad text.

## Phone number

Avoid adding your phone number in the ad. Your ad is likely to be disapproved by Google and won't run until you remove it. Their policy states that phone numbers should be only added in the call extension option. However, I've seen ads that have been approved with the phone number added in the headline or description of the ad. It really depends who has reviewed it at Google and not everyone over there seems to know about their own policies. At the very least, replicating your phone number leaves you less room to write your benefits, call to action, and message.

## The message

Avoid talking about yourself and how long you've been in business. Instead, talk about what the searcher is looking for and how they can benefit. Make sure you include a Unique Selling Point (USP) to differentiate your ad. For example, if you have a quick 30-minute turnaround that no one else can deliver, then include this prominently in the ad - and also in one of the headlines.

## Expanded text ads

Expanded text ads are the new format, released in the last 2-3 years. The benefit of this format is that ads now get more prominence in the search results above organic listings.

As an advertiser, you should use as much text space as possible to get your point across. Each line in the ad has a maximum amount of characters, so you have to be creative when creating headlines and descriptions. You don't have much space to play with. This calls for short pithy text that will make people take action.

These are the current character limits for each line:

Final URL

Headline 1 - 30 characters

Headline 2 - 30 characters

Headline 3 - 30 characters

Path 1 - 15 characters

Path 2 - 15 characters

Description 1 - 90 characters

Description 2 - 90 characters

Bear in mind this also includes spaces.

**New text ad**

Final URL                                        ⑦

Headline 1                                       ⑦
                                              0 / 30
Headline 2                                       ⑦
                                              0 / 30
Headline 3                                       ⑦
                                              0 / 30
Display path ⑦
www.example.com / Path 1        / Path 2
                        0 / 15              0 / 15

Description 1                                    ⑦

Each headline has a maximum of 30 characters. In headline one, I recommend adding the main keyword people use to find your product or service. It's one of the first things people see and they are more likely to click if they see the keyword in the ad.

In headline two, you should add your call to action. This is basically what you want them to do when they get to your website. So if you offer a quote, you can say something like 'Get Free Quote Now'.

Headline 3 is where you can add a benefit related to your product or service. Of course, you can rotate these three and place ads in a different format with the call to action in headline one and the keyword in headline two. The performance of each at auction time will tell you what people respond to the most.

## Responsive text ads

Responsive text ads are the latest major update to text ads.

The format of a responsive ad is similar to an expanded ad, except you have more options to add headlines and descriptions.

Whereas an expanded ad has a maximum of three headlines and up to two descriptions, a responsive ad has up to 15 headlines and up to 4 descriptions.

However, it's important to note that to a searcher on Google, there's no difference between an expanded text ad and a responsive ad - they look the same. The benefit with responsive ads is the headlines and descriptions are rotated by the machine learning system to show the most relevant and are targeted to the search query at auction time.

So, if possible, always create responsive ads and add as many headlines and descriptions as possible. You'll soon see an improvement in performance.

## Keyword Planner Tool

So, you've set up your first ad group and are ready to start advertising. But not quite yet. First, you should look at adding other keywords in their own ad groups. The best place to find them is with the Keyword Planner tool.

Of course, keyword research is an activity you can carry out before you set up any campaigns. This helps you see your keyword potential and helps you decide how much to spend.

When you've found a good list of keywords, you can group them according to themes and then set up ad groups for each of these themes.

You can access the Keyword Planner tool by clicking 'Tools & Settings' in the top right corner and under the 'Planning' section, click 'Keyword Planner'

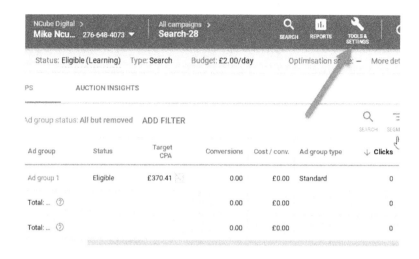

You can enter one or more keywords in the 'Find new keywords' section. Like the keyword research tool we used when setting up the first ad group, you can use either keywords or a URL related to your business to conduct the research.

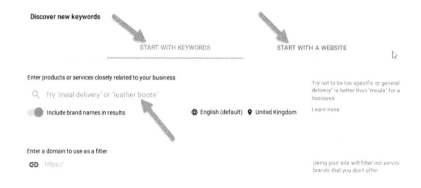

The report shows you a number of columns that help you decide which keywords to pick.

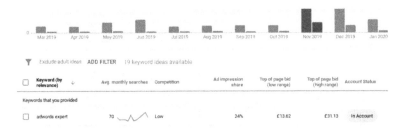

First, you'll see the results for the specific keywords you searched for. Below these, you'll see other keyword ideas that are closely related to your keywords.

Each keyword result has data to help you decide which ones to pick:

### Avg. Monthly Searches

This column shows the average monthly searches for your keyword and its close variants. You can use this to see how popular your keywords are and then plan your budgets.

### Competition

Competition reveals how competitive your keyword is in your targeted location and the search network targeting you've selected. Your keywords will have either low, medium, or high competition levels and this is determined by the number of advertisers in the auction and how aggressive they are. If Google Ads does not have enough data to calculate competition, you will see a dash (-) next to the keyword.

**Ad Impression Share**

This column will only show a result if the keyword is in the account and is receiving impressions. It shows the number of impressions you've received divided by the total number of searches for the location and network. It's expressed as a percentage and if there's not enough data for your keyword, you'll see a dash (-).

**Top of page bid (low range)**

This shows the lower range of what advertisers for the keyword have historically paid for a top of page bid. The actual cost per click (CPC) will vary.

## Top of page bid (high range)

This is significantly higher as you'll see in many reports. It shows the higher range of what advertisers have historically paid for a keyword top of the page bid.

## Account status

This tells you if the keyword is in the account or not.

Finally, you can select the keywords you want and add them directly to your campaign and ad groups or create new ad groups for them.

## Add Negative Keywords

Negative keywords are the opposite of the keywords you bid on. With normal keywords, you're looking to target search queries that are relevant to your business. But with negative keywords, you are looking to block irrelevant.

As part of your keyword research, you should also look out for keywords you can add as negatives. This will save you a lot of money because you won't get clicks from irrelevant searches and you'll have more to spend on relevant keywords.

Make a list of keywords you want to block and on the 'Negative Keywords' tab in your new campaign, under the Keywords section, click the blue '+' button and add them one per line in the box that opens. Then click 'Save'.

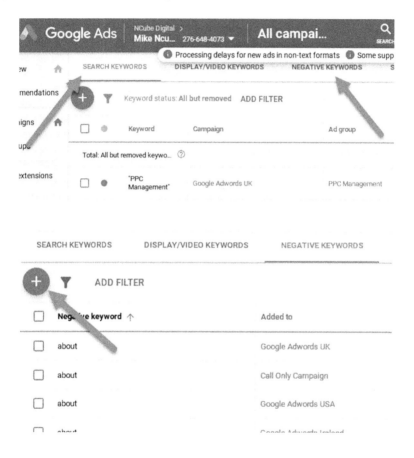

## Conversion Tracking Setup

Conversion tracking helps you track your campaign's performance. With tracking in place, you can see which ads and keywords are driving sales or enquiries to your business and which are underperforming.

There are 4 main options to choose from when setting up conversion tracking:

- Website - tracks sales, leads, and other actions on your website.

- App - tracks app installations and in-app actions if you have an app you're promoting.

- Phone calls - allows you to track calls from your ads or your website. So if someone clicks the Call option on your ad or clicks the phone number on your website, this will be recorded.

- Import - with this option you can, for example, track how many people bought your product from your store, if you have one.

The website option is the most applicable at this point. However, you should consider setting up goal conversions in Analytics and import them into your account. Call conversions are important too and you should set these up as early possible.

## Website conversion tracking setup

The first thing you need to do is decide which action you want to track on your website. Some popular options include a contact form, booking form, or lead enquiry form.

The setup of each of these will be very similar and you can usually use the same conversion action for all of them, but I would recommend you use a different setup for each form depending on what you want your visitors to do.

## Follow these instructions to set up conversion tracking for your website:

### 1. Click 'Tools & Settings' in the top right section.

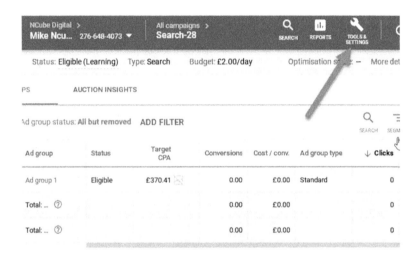

2. Under 'Measurement click 'Conversions'.

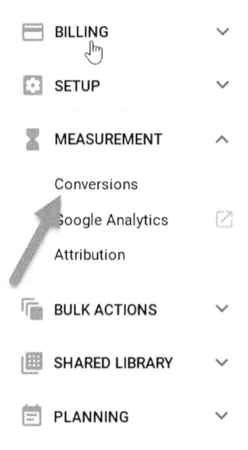

## 3. Click the blue '+' button.

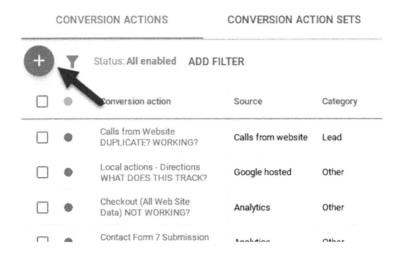

## 4. Click the website option to begin conversion tracking setup.

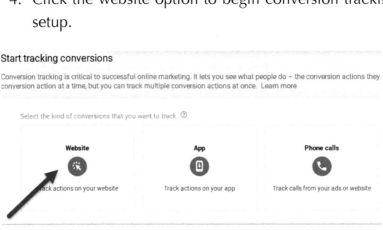

5. This will open 'create an action' where you can populate the various features for your conversion action.

6. Choose the category relevant to the action you want to track. Options include purchase, lead, page view, sign-up, and others. You can only select one.

7. Enter a name for the conversion action. It should easily make sense when you look at all the conversion actions in your account.

8. Add a value that helps you effectively analyse the impact of your advertising campaigns. This can be a bit tricky if each transaction has a different value but you should use the same value if you're tracking leads, sign-ups or page views. If you sell multiple products you can give each of them a different value and then add dynamic values to your tracking code on the next page. If you don't want to add a value, just select 'Don't add a value for this conversion'.

9. For the 'Count' option, if you're tracking leads or sign-ups then select 'One' because only the first interaction is valuable. On the other hand, if you want to track

sales, then use the default 'Every' to track every sale because every sale is valuable.

10. Next, click 'Create and Continue' to move to the next stage.

11. You've now created a conversion action and you just need to set up the tag to add to your website.

12. You have three options here: 1. Install the tag yourself, 2. Email the tag to your webmaster, or 3. Use Google Tag Manager. Select the best option for you. If you're new to this then it's likely you need to email it to your webmaster or web developer.

**Go Live!**

Congratulations! You've set up your first Google Ads campaign and you're now ready to start advertising. Your ads will go through a review process, which will take up to 24 hours but is usually much quicker than that and could be ready in an hour.

When your ads are live on Google you can carry out a search to see what they look like. However, try to not search on Google for your ads because that increases your impression count and reduces your click-through rate (CTR). You're unlikely to click on your own ads.

Instead, use the 'Ad Preview and Diagnosis' tool that's in your Google Ads account. You will find this in the 'Tools' section of your account next to Keyword Planner under .the Tools & Settings section

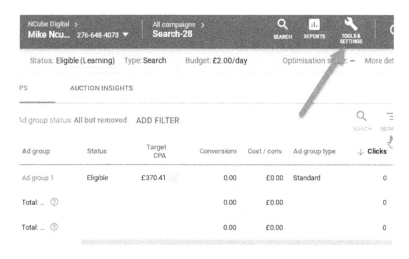

To start, enter a search term you want to check your ads against. It will give you some suggestions based on keywords in your campaign and you can pick one of them to conduct a search.

You can also update the location you want to check and this is one of the main benefits of this tool, as you can see what your ads look like in different locations. For example, if you're targeting Paris and you are in the UK, the tool will show you what your ads look like for people in Paris. You normally won't see this when you use Google to check your ads.

You can also use the tool to see what your ads look like on mobile, desktop, and tablet devices.

Another reason why you should use this tool instead of a Google search is that it will tell you the reason why your ad is not showing for a particular search term. Maybe your ad is not showing because it is under review, the budget has run out, the ad rank is low or another reason. You are likely to see this in the Ad Preview and Diagnosis tool.

## Summary

Keyword selection is the most important part of setting up a Google Ads campaign. It helps you identify the best keywords that will drive targeted search queries from your target market.

You could start keyword research before you set up your campaign settings or when you reach the ad group setup stage, as we have done here. Either option works and depends on the nature of your business. If you're not sure your business model works on Google Ads, then it may be best to carry out keyword research first, because that will save you a lot of wasted time if you choose not to advertise.

# SECTION TWO

## Introduction

So, you've set up your first campaign, launched it and it's now running. You are likely getting traffic and impressions and clicks continue to increase.

Now we come to the other important part of advertising on Google - management.

It's not enough to set up a good, targeted campaign. You need to manage and optimise the campaign to be able to achieve your goals.

Your competitors will be setting up new campaigns and updating them in line with performance and how you are also managing yours. They will also be updating their bid strategies to outrank you and other competitors, so it's important you update yours too.

Google also releases new updates regularly and you should keep up with these and implement them as they become available.

One of the common questions I get from advertisers is how much time and work is required to manage their campaigns. The truth is you need to spend as much time as possible to make it happen. Of course, this depends on the size of the account, how much you are spending, and the industry you are in.

In this section, we will look at all the important features to help you manage your campaign effectively and spend only one hour each week doing it.

# CHAPTER 8

# Week 1 (1 hour)

## Introduction

Week 1 is when you begin optimising the campaign based on performance. This can be after a week or month of running the ads so you can get sufficient traffic volumes to be able to assess performance. It's important you allow the ads to run and accrue sufficient click volume before making changes.

The time between launching your campaign and starting the management can vary. It can be a few days or a few weeks later and it really depends on the volume of traffic you've received.

For example, if you run a service business you may want to wait until you have between 50-100 clicks before starting management. On the other hand, for an e-commerce business selling clothing 300 clicks is usually sufficient traffic to assess performance.

## Search Terms Analysis

The search terms report is one of the most important reports in Google Ads. It shows the actual searches that drove impressions and clicks for your ads.

You can see this report at the keyword level for your campaigns and ad groups. You can also change the date range to see which search terms you received for different periods such as today, yesterday, the last 30 days, the last month and so on.

One of the things you'll notice is there are many more searches than the keywords you have in your campaigns or ad groups. In some cases, you can see thousands of search terms in this report for just a few keywords depending on your industry and nature of business.

You can customise the report to your requirements, so you can add and remove columns to assess each search term's performance. The keyword column is not added by default so you can add it to the report here.

Adding the keyword column and moving it closer to the search term column is so you can see which keywords triggered which term. This helps you to quickly see how targeted your keywords and match types are and if you need to stop any.

Another important set of columns are your conversion metrics, which include conversions, conversion rate, and cost/conversion.

## Add Negative Keywords

This will be one of the most important activities you carry out each month as you manage your campaign. The search terms report we've discussed above will help you identify search queries that are not relevant for your business.

It would be great if you could identify all of the irrelevant keywords before you even start advertising. This would save you a lot of money and time, of course, and make your campaign profitable very early.

However, this is not possible. People search on Google in all kinds of ways and it's impossible to have a comprehensive list before you start advertising. According to Google, 15% of searches are completely new.

It's impossible to find any of these searches during a normal keyword research exercise because they won't appear. However, many of these are long-tail searches and you'll find many will bring you the best conversions - so it's important that you're targeting them.

You'll also see many keywords that are not relevant and you should block these so they don't trigger your ads.

Adding negative keywords is quick and easy and you can select any you want to add directly to the campaign. You can also add them at the ad group level or to a negative keyword list you've created or you can create a list at that point.

Negative keyword lists save you a lot of time because as your account grows and you add more campaigns, you can quickly assign negative lists to them.

Without a negative list, it means you will have to add negative keywords in the new campaigns individually, which can cause errors and wastes time.

You can see all the negative lists in your account by clicking Tools > Negative keyword lists.

The search terms report essentially shows you which searches are relevant and which aren't. The relevant ones you can add as keywords if they are not in there already and the irrelevant you can add as negative keywords.

To add any search term as a negative keyword, select it and then click 'Add as negative keyword', then select the option to add it to the campaign. You can also select to add it to the specific ad group, but that means any other ad group may still be able to trigger that search term if it has related keywords.

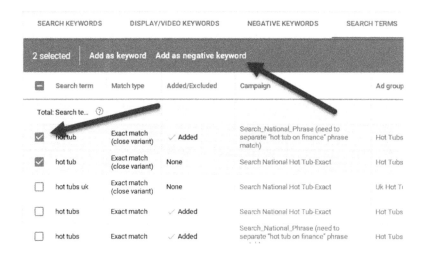

Which negative keywords you add is important too. For example, you will see some long-tail searches with 4 or more words in them and adding the whole search query will not be effective.

Instead, you want to add the specific word in the search term that is not relevant for your ads. For example, a maths tutor for children will have words such as 'become a maths tutor'. This search would not be relevant, because the tutor is only looking to target people looking for maths lessons and not to become a tutor.

So adding this as a negative keyword would be a good idea. However, instead of adding the whole search phrase 'become a maths tutor', it would be better to only add the word 'become' as a negative keyword.

The benefit here is that this will block all future searches with the word 'become' such as:

- How to become a maths tutor

- Steps to become a maths tutor

## Click-through Rate (CTR) Analysis

There are many metrics to track in Google Ads and you can see them in your reports. These metrics tell you how your campaigns, ad groups, ads, keywords and so on are performing for you. Without them, you won't be able to manage your ads effectively and you could be losing a lot of money.

Some metrics will be more important to you than others and you will keep a close watch on them every month.

CTR is one of the key metrics. It's also one of the easiest to understand. CTR is the ratio of searchers that can view your ad to the total number of searchers that click your ad. It is expressed as a percentage.

| Campaign | | CTR | Avg. cost |
|---|---|---|---|
| t removed campaigns ⑦ | | 3.86% | £10.07 |
| 🔍 Google Adwords UK | | 3.66% | £10.84 |
| 🔍 Brand Searches | | 12.64% | £0.06 |
| 🔍 Digital Marketing Templates \| English Countries | | — | — |
| 🖽 Remarketing | | — | — |
| ▢ Video | | — | — |

The CTR formula is:

CTR = clicks divided by impressions.

For example, if your ad has received 100 impressions and had 10 clicks from that, then your CTR is 10%. Whether this is a good CTR or not depends on a number of factors.

A good click-through rate (CTR) in Google Ads is only possible when ads are relevance to searches. If searchers find your ads related to what they're searching for, they'll click.

However, there are many reasons why CTR may be low or high. A good CTR will vary between industries and will depend on factors such as ad position, campaign type, search intent, keyword type, device used and others. So it's not always easy to determine what a good CTR is. However, the following points should help to explain this better.

**Below 1% CTR**

CTRs below 1% are common for Display and Remarketing campaigns. This is because people are on websites that are part of the Google Display Network and aren't actively searching for your products or services. They will be checking out other content and are likely to ignore your image ads.

This is not necessarily a bad thing. Traffic volumes are usually higher for display campaigns and it's expected the vast majority of people will not click your image ads. The people who click are usually highly qualified leads and these are the ones you're interested in.

For search campaigns, CTRs below 1% aren't good. They reveal that your ads are not targeted to the searcher or they are appearing at the bottom of search results.

So, aim to rank higher by improving quality scores and also bidding higher for keywords. Keywords with high Ad Rank generally have higher CTRs. They also help to increase clicks and conversions and help you to quickly see what works or doesn't.

## Between 1-5% CTR

Achieving CTRs between 1-5% is a good target for a new campaign. It's a good place to start and with time and additional optimisation, this should be improved.

This CTR is common for shopping campaigns and many search campaigns with targeted ads. One way to improve these CTRs is to check the search terms report and remove any that aren't targeted or have low conversions.

## Above 5% CTR

If you're a charity using a Google Ad Grant, you'll need to maintain a minimum of 5% CTR for your account. This is a new requirement for all charities running campaigns on Google Ads.

Failure to maintain this means your account will be suspended. Google has taken this step because of advertisers abusing the free funding.

The challenge though is that you can't bid higher than £2. So your ads may not achieve top positions and that's usually required to have a high CTR.

The first step will be to remove all low CTR keywords and search terms, especially one-word keywords. Then carry out keyword research to find new long-tail keywords that are targeted and will help you maintain that target.

For all other advertisers, achieving 5% CTR is not a must, but it is a good target to aim for. It ensures your ads are targeted and people are interested in what you have to offer.

You can achieve this by bidding for higher positions and appearing in the top 3 positions. You can also optimise ads that have low CTRs.

**Above 10% CTR**

CTRs above 10% are great and are a sign of highly targeted ads.

These are common for businesses that offer services and target a local audience. These might be businesses such as an accountancy business, local tradesmen, legal services, and others that offer one or a few services with fewer searches to target, so it's easy to know what they're looking for.

## 20%+ CTR

Click through rates above 20% are common with brand searches. People searching for a product brand, service brand, or personality brand are likely to click through because they know exactly what they're looking for.

You'll see this if you bid on your brand name as above. However, if you're already ranking highly for your brand name and no one is bidding on it, then you should not bid on your brand name as this would be wasted spend. These searchers can easily click on your organic listing and still come through to your website.

CTRs above 20% are rare for general searches. There's usually a lot of competition and searchers have many advertisers to choose from. Your ads are also unlikely to be highly targeted for general searches so you'll get fewer clicks.

## How to fix a low CTR

Improving your Google Ads click-through rate (CTR) has many benefits, including:

1. Increases traffic volumes – when more people click your ads you then have more visitors which brings many benefits.

2. Increases conversions – with more visitors you then get more sales and leads because you have more potential customers.

3. Improves quality scores – this is one of the three quality score factors and when you improve Google Ads CTR, your scores increase too.

4. Higher Ad Rank – your ads are rewarded with higher positions when they are relevant to searches.

Achieving a good CTR should be every advertiser's goal. You should continue to work on your targeting, ads, keywords, search terms, bids, positions, and more to improve click-through rates.

**Follow these tips to improve your Google Ads CTR:**

**Gain Top Positions**

A top position on Google is a placement in one of the top 4 positions in the auction results. Ads that are at the top get significantly higher CTRs than those at the bottom – below organic results.

There are two main ways to gain top positions on Google: increase your bids and improve ad quality. Improving ad quality takes longer because you have to work on your ad relevance and ensure that keywords are tightly themed in the ad groups and related to text ads.

Increasing bids is a lot quicker to do. You can increase bids manually if you're using a manual bid strategy or use an automated strategy to outrank competitors.

**Remove Low CTR Keywords**

Check your campaigns for keywords with low CTRs. If your target is to have a minimum of 5% CTR and some are as low as 1% or lower and with poor performance for conversions too, then you should remove them.

Trying to improve these won't help. It will waste time, which you could use to focus on better-performing keywords.

## Remove Low CTR Search Terms

Check the search terms report to look for low performing searches. If they have low CTRs and conversions are low too, then you can remove them by adding them as negative keywords.

It's not surprising to find search terms with CTRs as high as 100%. That's because search terms tend to be much higher in number than your keywords. People search in all kinds of ways and one keyword can trigger hundreds of search terms.

Many of these will have high CTRs. However, some will have low CTRs and these you can remove. Doing so will help to improve keyword click-through rates and overall performance.

## Remove Low CTR Ads

Each of your Ad groups should have between 3-5 ads for testing purposes. When the ad group is active, you'll see the click-through rate for each ad and over time you'll see the best and least performing ones.

You can also replace low performing ads with better-performing ones

## Add Ad Extensions

Ad extensions give your ads more prominence in search results. Adding many ad extensions helps to push your ads to the top as they become more relevant to searchers. Searchers are then more likely to click through, so try to add as many sitelinks, callout, structured snippet, call, price, and location extensions as you can.

## Include Keywords in the Text Ad

Add the keyword in the ad. The best place to add it is in the headline, and Headline 1 in particular. This is the most prominent part of the ad and the clickable part that takes the visitor to your landing page.

People are more likely to click when they see their keyword in the ad. They'll perceive the ad to be relevant to what they need and they'll find this on the landing page.

Of course, each ad group will have multiple keywords - each ad group should have at least 5. This then makes it difficult to have every keyword included in the ad.

The solution is to use Dynamic Keyword Insertion (DKI). This syntax replaces the default text you add with the searcher's keyword (bear in mind it's the keyword and not the search term that is included).

This is what the Dynamic Keyword Insertion syntax looks like:

{keyWord:Default Ad Text}

Read more about Dynamic Keyword Insertion here https://support.google.com/Google Ads/answer/74992?hl=en-GB

**Make Ads Relevant**

The DKI syntax mentioned above is one way to make Ads relevant. Another way is to add key benefits and a unique selling point to entice visitors to click. It also differentiates your ads from competitors.

Many ads in search results are drowning in a sea of sameness. They look like many others on the page and aren't differentiated in any way, so searchers click on any they see because there's nothing to differentiate them.

From now on, study what your competitors are promoting. Then look for ways on how to make your ads different by presenting your benefits and unique selling point.

**Summary**

CTR, as we've discussed in this chapter, is one of the most important metrics. It's a basic metric for sure and easy to calculate, however, it tells you a lot about how your ads, keywords, and campaigns have performed.

As a basic metric, it helps you delve deeper into your reports to gain a greater understanding of how your campaign is performing.

The search terms report is one of the most important reports in your account. It helps you see what searches you've actually received and you should look at this report every week.

The search terms report is where you'll see irrelevant searches you should add as negative keywords. Adding negatives helps to improve the efficiency of your ads and reduces your cost per acquisition.

# CHAPTER 9

# Week 2 (1 hour)

## Introduction

In week 2, you will now have more data to be able to assess reports effectively. You will also know which assets are working for you and which aren't so conversion metrics will be key to assessing reports and optimising the campaign.

Some of these metrics include conversion rate, cost per conversion, and total conversions and can be viewed at the campaign, ad group, ad, and keyword level.

This information helps you to optimise your ads effectively and add or remove new ones accordingly.

You can also update ad extensions like sitelinks, callouts, and structured snippets based on conversion data. Just make sure you have sufficient data to make that possible.

## Conversion Tracking Analysis

There are a number of reasons why your conversion tracking isn't working. I've listed some of the main ones here:

## Conversion Tracking Not Set Up

If you cannot see any conversion data then it's possible it hasn't been set up. If your reports show zero figures for the following metrics, then it may have not been set up correctly or at all:

- Conversion

- Cost Per Conversion

- Conversion Rate

## Tracking Code Not Installed

One of the main reasons why conversion tracking isn't working is because the code hasn't been installed. Setting it up in Google Ads is only half the job - you also need to add the tracking code on your 'success' or 'thank you' page that people see when they fill out a form on your website.

It's advisable to add the tracking code as soon as you set up conversion tracking, that way you're unlikely to forget.

You can also check the tracking page source code to see if it has been added successfully. Check between the head tag of the page, which is where it should be added.

In WordPress, some plugins can help you easily add tracking codes. Check they are compatible with your version of WordPress and check the reviews to assess how good they are before downloading any.

**Installed in the Wrong Place**

If you install the tracking code in the wrong place, you won't have any conversion data. If the code hasn't been added between the head tag in your source code then it's unlikely to trigger when people complete a conversion action on your website.

**Conversions Not Imported**

If you've set up goals but have not imported them into Google Ads then you won't have any conversion tracking.

When your Google Ads and Analytics accounts are linked you can import goals into Google Ads and set up conversion tracking this way. This is a straightforward process that allows you to see how your campaigns are performing.

## Remove Low Performing Assets

Your campaign reports will reveal how each ad, keyword, and search query is working for your business. You'll be able to see what click-through rates, conversions, clicks, and impressions each of these assets receive.

| Campaign | CTR | Avg. cost | ↓ Cost | Conversions | Cost / conv. | Conv. rate |
|---|---|---|---|---|---|---|
| moved campaigns ⓘ | 3.86% | £10.07 | £1,540.40 | 5.00 | £308.08 | 3.27% |
| 🔍 Google Adwords UK | 3.66% | £10.84 | £1,539.69 | 5.00 | £307.94 | 3.52% |
| 🔍 Brand Searches | 12.64% | £0.06 | £0.71 | 0.00 | £0.00 | 0.00% |

With this information, you're now able to remove any that are performing badly and improve some that just need updating.

For example, your search terms report which you can see in the Keywords tab reveals all the searches that have triggered your ads. As noted in Chapter 8, this report is one of the most important for your search campaign and you should regularly analyse it.

For your text ads, one of the easiest metrics to track is the click-through rate (CTR). You can see it for all the ads in the campaign, and in each ad group, you'll have between 3-5 ads where you can compare one ad CTR to another.

## Ad Extensions Optimisation

In the 'Ads & extensions' tab, you'll see the 'extensions' tab where you can see performance results for your ad extensions.

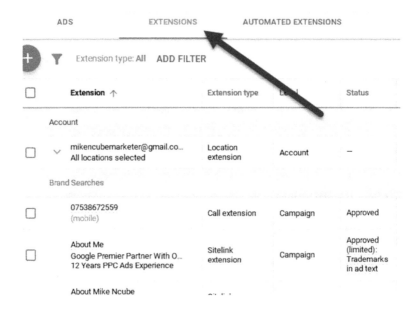

Here you can see all your extensions like sitelinks, callouts, call, structured snippets and so on. Next to each, you'll see the status and the metrics which reveal how each has been performing.

You will see impressions, clicks, CTR, average CPC, and others for each extension and you can add or update them according to performance. If you find the CTR is at 1.3% for a sitelink, for example, you can either update it or remove it altogether.

There are at least 5 clickable extensions and the 2 main ones are: sitelinks and call extensions. You'll see the clicks for these when you segment your reports in the campaign section.

Click the 'Segment' link and then click the 'Click Type' link and you will see the reports for your extensions.

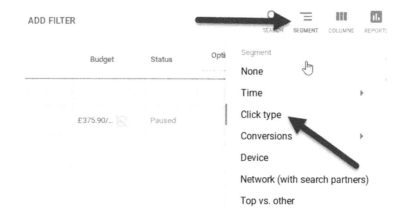

**Summary**

In this chapter we have covered the actions you will take in week 2 to improve your campaign. This includes updating and removing low performing adverts to improve CTRs, conversion rates, and other key metrics.

It also includes optimising ad extensions in line with performance and adding new ones as they become available.

We've also looked at conversion tracking analysis to see how your ads and keywords are performing. These are some of your most important metrics and could determine the success or failure of your campaign.

# CHAPTER 10

# Week 3 (1 hour)

## Introduction

In week 3 you will focus on adding more keywords through keyword research to increase search volume and conversions. Using the Keyword Planner tool, you'll conduct some research on your products or services to find additional keywords you can add in your ad groups and bid on.

Because you will add some new keywords, this will also be a good time to increase your budget. Usually, more keywords mean more traffic which means more costs, so you should tap into this by increasing the budget.

It's also an important time to increase your budget because you will now have a comprehensive negative list and your searches are more targeted. This means there's less likely to be any wastage.

Adding new keywords will also require some ad changes, especially if you decide to promote other products or services.

You may have to create new ad groups with separate ads and keywords to bid on.

The recommendations section in your account will give you some ideas for keywords, ads, and budget ideas to implement. This is based on Google's machine learning system and is specific to your campaign, but don't just implement the suggestions, first check that they are applicable and then implement if you are happy.

## Campaign Recommendations

The 'Recommendations' tab is available for all your campaigns. In this section, you can see a list of opportunities Google Ads has identified as being relevant to your campaign.

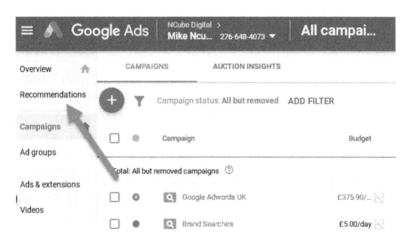

You can review each recommendation and ultimately the decision is yours whether to implement it or not. If you find a recommendation you believe is relevant and could help improve your campaign, then you can click 'Apply' to accept and implement it.

For any recommendations that are not relevant, you can either ignore or discard them from the recommendation list so they do not appear again.

Each campaign in your account has a 'Campaign Optimisation Score' which is an estimate of how well your campaign is set to perform. Your aim is to bring your score up to 100% and maintain it by applying recommendations or discarding them if they are not relevant.

This score runs from 0% to 100% with 100% meaning that your campaign can perform at its full potential. You'll see a list of recommendations that can help you optimise your campaign and next to each you'll see how much your optimisation score will be impacted (in percentages) when you apply that recommendation.

## Recommendations

Your optimisation score ⑦

Improve your score by following recomn

# 95%

**ALL RECOMMENDATIONS**  ( REPAIRS )

Score for Search, Display and Shopping
campaigns

Some common recommendations you'll find as you manage your campaigns are:

- Bid more efficiently with Target CPA - this gets you more conversions at a lower rate or similar CPA with a fully automated bid strategy. This is recommended because Google shows your campaigns are likely to benefit from Target CPA bidding.

- Add new keywords - there will be new keyword suggestions here that you can add to show your ads more often to people searching for your business offer. This is recommended because you are not targeting searches that could be relevant to your business.

- Raise your budgets - your ads have stopped running on your busiest days and fixing your limited budget can help.

- Create dynamic search ads - show your ads on searches relevant to your business that you may be missing with your keyword-based ad groups. This is recommended because you can drive additional traffic with Dynamic Search Ads that includes the suggested landing pages.

Bear in mind that not all of these will be relevant for your campaigns, so you can remove them. You can then focus on the most relevant. Any recommendations you implement should be monitored to see what impact they've had on the campaign's performance.

**Conduct Keyword Research**

Conducting Google keyword research is one of the first tasks you should do as part of setting up a Google Ads campaign. It will help you find the right keywords to bid on.

You'll save a lot of money by not bidding on irrelevant keywords. Bidding on the wrong keywords can be costly and is one main reason why many campaigns fail.

The Keyword Planner Tool in Google Ads is one of the best keyword research tools to help you achieve your goals. It's a free tool and has many impressive features. One of them is the ability to forecast the potential of your keywords and then add them directly to your account.

Google Ads keyword research is a key part of setting up successful Pay Per Click campaigns. It's one of the first things you'll do and you should spend enough time researching to find the various ways people search for your products or services.

First, you should understand your customers' needs. Try to think of all the ways they'll search and make a list of popular keywords you can use as part of your research.

Then go over to the Keyword Planner Tool to start the search. This is a free tool in your Google Ads account and it will show you a lot of information about your keywords, including:

- What traffic volumes they get each month.

- Closely related keywords you can add.

- Suggested bids based on past performance.

- How competitive they are – low, medium or high competition.

- What budgets you should consider setting.

- Suggested campaign and ad group grouping according to themes.

So there's a lot you can see from your Google Ads keyword research and here are some reasons why it's important:

**Find good keywords**

Before doing any keyword research, it's fairly simple to find up to 3 keywords that represent what you do. Most people can do this easily, however, you need a more extensive list to target the various ways people search.

The Google Keyword Planner Tool will help you find keywords to bid on. These keywords will be based on the products or services you sell and they'll cover the various ways that people search on Google.

Some will not be relevant, of course, but it's important to identify them so you can add them as negative keywords. Negative keyword research is as important as keyword research because it reveals the searches that would be a waste of your budget.

## Estimation of traffic volumes

Google Ads keyword research will show you the average number of monthly searches for your keywords. This shows how many impressions your ads would have received and you can also work out the number of clicks based on bids and click through rates.

This helps with your Google Ads budget setting. It would be a challenge to know what budgets to assign to your campaigns without knowing the number of impressions and potential clicks you could get.

The suggested bid also gives you an indication of competition level. If the suggested bid is high, then you have to assign a higher budget to get decent click volumes.

## Estimation of costs

The Keyword Planner Tool has an inbuilt forecasting tool. You should use this tool when you've created a good list of keywords and now need to know what costs you're likely to pay.

You can adjust your keyword bids to see what click volume will be and at what cost. This helps you plan your keyword strategy and also enables you to remove keywords that may prove too expensive at the beginning.

## Discover competitor strategy

Competitor tools aren't available in Google Ads, but there are some third-party tools like Spyfu and SE Ranking that help you to discover your competitor's ads and keywords.

You will see a lot of information from these tools, including:

- Top or bottom rankings for each keyword they are bidding on.

- How much they are paying on average for each keyword.

- What specific ads are showing for their keywords.

- How much they are spending on their Google Ads campaigns.

- What the competition levels are like for their keywords.

## Update Campaign Budget

As a Google Ads Expert, one question I'm always asked by clients is what they should be spending on their campaigns.

Of course, most advertisers prefer to start with as little as possible, and this is understandable, especially in the beginning when you're unlikely to know how your ads will perform.

Your Google Ads Budget is set at the account or campaign level. The campaign level option is the most common and it's where you state the maximum amount you'd like to spend.

Setting this is pretty straightforward. Go to the campaign you'd like to add or update a budget for and click 'settings'. In the budget section, add the amount that you'd like to spend per day.

You can also set budgets at the account level. You can do this in the shared library section and create a budget portfolio you can assign to one or more campaigns. This is the main advantage of using an account level budget because it saves you a lot of time and helps you manage budgets easier.

To arrive at your daily Google Ads Budget, take your monthly budget and divide it by 30.4. So, if you're looking to spend £3,000 per month in your campaign, you'll divide that by 30.4 to arrive at a £98.68 daily budget. (30.4 is the average number of days in a month).

This is assuming you want to advertise on all days of the month, however, if you'd like to advertise on working days only, for example, then that would be about 22 days your ads will be active. Your £3,000 monthly budget will then equate to a £136 daily budget.

However, there's a difference between budget and spend. Your budget is the maximum you want to put towards promoting your products or services on Google. Spend is the actual amount you're charged in your campaign.

It's possible to have a high budget but spend a very low amount. For example, if you have a monthly Google Ads budget of £2,000 and you only spend £800. This can happen if there aren't sufficient impressions and clicks to use up all the budget or if ads are ranked low and appear at the bottom of the page or on page 2 and beyond.

It's also possible to have a budget but overshoot it when traffic volumes are high. This will happen only daily, but you'll not be charged more than your monthly Google Ads budget. Google allows this overshoot, to help advertisers get quality traffic when it's most important and it also ensures you're always close to your maximum limit, as some days are likely to be quieter.

**Summary**

In this chapter, we've looked at the updates you'll need to do in week 3 of management to improve the performance of your campaign. This includes exploring the recommendations to get suggestions from Google on how to improve key areas of your campaign.

We've also looked at how you can find new keyword opportunities by conducting additional keyword research using the Keyword Planner tool.

This is the time when you should consider increasing your budget to increase traffic and sales. This is especially important if you've done your keyword research and added some new keywords.

# CHAPTER 11

# Week 4 (1 hour)

## Introduction

Week 4 concludes the first full month of managing your campaign. You have a well-optimised campaign that should be bringing in some sales or leads by now.

Many of your keywords should now have quality score data so you can gain some greater analysis on your campaigns. We will focus on improving your campaign quality to get your keywords closer to a 10/10 quality score.

This also requires you to analyse your landing pages to improve engagement and reduce bounce rates. As you will see, it's not enough that you create quality ads and keywords to target the right people, only to have a poor or average landing page experience. You need to create a great user experience too.

We will delve into your auction insights report to see who your direct competitors are and how competitive your ads are against theirs. This will help you update your bidding strategy so your ads are more competitive.

## Quality Score Analysis

Quality score is a diagnostic tool that reveals the health of your ads and landing pages. It's reported for every keyword in your account that has had sufficient impressions and clicks.

So, any keyword that has not run or has had few impressions and clicks won't have a quality score. Instead, it will be reported as a null quality score and will have the symbol '-'' next to it.

Generally, quality scores above 6/10 are good and reveal that the ads and landing pages are optimised. A 10/10 quality score is excellent and what you should be aiming for.

When user experience is good, it then it's good for everyone: for advertisers, Google, and the user too.

There are three main factors to quality score you should work on to improve:

- Expected Click Through Rate (CTR)
- Ad Relevance

- Landing Page Experience

Each of these factors is more important than the quality score number you see for the keyword. The quality score is an aggregate of these three factors and doesn't in itself tell you as much as each of the contributing factors.

Google is always looking for ways to improve the way quality score is calculated. That calculation will never be captured by a simple 1 – 10 number – which is why they call it a guide and not a precise metric.

Other factors contribute to ad quality that aren't directly reflected in quality score, these are:

- Geographic Signals – the country of the search will affect ad quality.

- User Device – the device, whether it's desktop, tablet or mobile, will determine ad quality. This is taken into account when ad quality is calculated and it's important your site is optimised for mobile visitors. Try targeting mobile visitors with specific mobile-friendly ads and pages.

You can see the quality scores for your keywords by customising the data table reports and adding a quality score column.

| | SEARCH | SEGM | COLUMNS | REPORTS | DOWNLOAD | EXPAND | MORE |
|---|---|---|---|---|---|---|---|

| ↓ Clicks | Modify columns | | Avg. CPC | Cost |
|---|---|---|---|---|
| 14 | Your column sets | | £10.84 | £1,539.69 |
| 23 | Custom | | £13.54 | £311.36 |
| 12 | 95 | 12.63% | £12.58 | £150.91 |
| 10 | 93 | 10.75% | £11.83 | £118.33 |

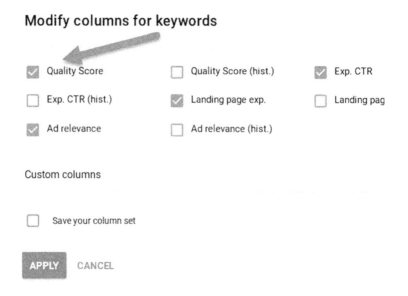

## Modify columns for keywords

Some tips to improve quality scores for your keywords are:

### Improve Landing Pages

Landing pages are where people end up when they've clicked your ads. They should be relevant to the search terms they've used and the keywords in the ad groups as well as the offer you've promised them in the ad.

Landing page experience is clearly an important quality score factor. You want to make sure that bounce rates are low and that people are engaged when they're on your website.

To reduce bounce rates, you should have visitors visit other related pages on your site. For example, if you want people to contact you, make sure you add a contact form which sends them to a 'Thank You' page when they've clicked the 'Submit' button.

Doing this will reduce bounce rates and you can keep visitors more engaged by providing another related offer on the thank you page that moves them further down the buying funnel.

This also helps to set expectations. You can state on the landing page when your visitor can expect to hear from you and how you'll be contacting them.

On the other hand, if you have a contact form and all visitors see when they click the submit button is an online message which says something like 'thanks for your message' you'll need to change this and add a thank you page instead.

**Increase Click-Through Rate**

The click-through rate formula is displayed as a percentage and is calculated by dividing clicks by impressions.

It's a measure of how targeted your ads are. If ads are targeted to the right audience then you'll see good CTRs. This will depend on your industry and it will vary for different keyword types.

However, 5% is usually a good CTR. That means for every one hundred people that see your ads, 5 click through to your website. Other factors will also come into play such as competitors and their offers and where you're ranking in the ad auction results.

However, quality score is decided by expected CTR and it forecasts what the CTR will be based on past performance, device used, search terms used, location of the searcher, and other factors.

There're a number of ways to improve click-through rate, including:

1. Ensuring the keyword is included in the ad –the headline in particular.

2. Using the Dynamic Keyword Insertion syntax to include the keyword in the ad automatically.

3. Removing ads, keywords and search terms with low CTRs.

4. Removing broad match type keywords.

5. Removing one-word keywords that are underperforming.

**Make Ads Relevant**

Making ads relevant is the most important factor to improve quality score. When people search and see the ad is what they've been looking for, they'll click through to learn more.

Google is serious about ad relevance. Over the years they've updated the algorithms to reward ads that are relevant to searches and quality score is one of the most important metrics they've implemented to show how relevant ads are to keywords.

Ad relevance is about ensuring the following:

- The keyword used is included in the Ad text.

- The product or service searched for is mentioned in the Ad.

- All relevant ad extensions have been added.

- Character limit has been reached.

## Add Ad Extensions

Ad Extensions give your ad more prominence in the search results. Your ad gets more space when you include all applicable sitelinks, callouts, call, price, structured snippet and location extensions.

People are more likely to click through when your ad is at the top, and this increases your CTR and quality score.

## Target the Right Search Terms

Targeting the right search terms helps to boost your keyword quality scores. If search terms aren't related to your ads and the products or services you're promoting, then quality scores will be low.

As we've discussed previously, there's a difference between a keyword and a search term. A keyword is what you add in your campaign to target people who are looking for your products or services. A search term is what people use to find your products or services. The match types are what match your ads to the user's search terms.

Keyword match types control the search terms that trigger your ads. To reiterate, the four match types you can use are broad, modified broad, phrase, and exact match.

Each ad group can have one or more keyword match types. When you first launch your PPC campaigns, it's usually best not to add broad match keywords because they target a broad range of searches and some may not be relevant. This is mainly because building a comprehensive list of negative keywords takes a while and you need them to block all irrelevant searches.

It's best to start with phrase, exact, or modified broad match keywords. They allow you to control the search types you get while you build your negative list.

When you've built a good list of negative keywords, you can look to increase your reach by targeting many long-tail keywords with broad match type keywords.

## Landing Page Analysis

A landing page is a page on your website visitors reach when they click one of your ads. Its goal is to deliver on what your ad has promised the visitor and should provide a great user experience for them too.

Landing page experience is one of the three main factors behind your quality scores. If you have high bounce rates and low visitor engagement this will show in your quality scores as a 'Below Average' landing page experience.

A poor landing page experience for your Google Ads visitors also means you are unlikely to achieve good conversion rates that would make advertising on Google worth it.

Below are 10 tips to help optimise your landing page experience and boost your Google Ads campaigns:

## Avoid popups

If you can, avoid adding popups, especially if they do not match the content on the landing page. Popups can be annoying for users and are usually not relevant for PPC campaigns because in most cases everything the visitor needs should be available on the landing page.

Google will also disapprove ads if a popup distracts visitors and is not relevant to the ad or keyword.

A popup can be okay if you want to highlight a special offer, like a discount voucher, that's related to the product or service on the landing page. This can actually lead to higher conversion rates because it can be a strong incentive for visitors.

Popups are also more of an annoyance on mobile devices because they are harder to close. One option is to have it appear for your desktop visitors and not mobile visitors. Mobile visitors usually have less time and patience and will quickly click the back button if they are obstructed.

**Remove all distractions**

Don't stop your visitors from doing what they have arrived on your landing page to do. Remember, they have clicked one of your ads and you have been charged by Google, so this should motivate you to make the experience as best as possible.

One common distraction is having too much text on a landing page. Most visitors don't read website text but just scan through it to pick the most important points. So if you have too much text on the page this could be off-putting for many people and will make it difficult for them to scan and find what they need.

Popups and banners can be distractions too and should be avoided at all costs. If you have to add them, they should be kept to a minimum and relevant to the page content and offers.

## Add a call to action

A call to action is a definite must for all your PPC landing pages. The call to action on your ad should be the same one visitors see on the landing page. So if the ad has promised a white paper download, this should be easily available on the landing page without the visitor having to search the website for it.

The call to action should also be visible - generally 'above the fold', which is what visitors see as soon as they land on the page.

This is especially important on mobile devices, which are harder to navigate than a desktop. Your conversion rates will be higher when the call to action is visible at the top on mobile devices – without visitors having to scroll down to see the call to action.

Many features can act as a call to action and these include a phone number, banner, email, form, button, and others.

## Use software like Hotjar

Hotjar is an amazing analytics platform developed in 2014 that helps you analyse your website traffic, receive feedback, carry out surveys and do much more to optimise your website and landing pages.

One of the best features is recording website visitor actions, which gives you an overview of how to improve your site's user experience, performance, and conversion rates.

## Use white space

Break up your text with white space to make it easier for your visitors to scan or read easily. There is nothing as off-putting on a landing page as large chunks of paragraphs with very little white space in between.

Visitors will find it hard to digest your content and will completely ignore anything that looks difficult to read, so you will fail to get your key points across and completely lose them to competitor sites that have well-structured content.

**Add reviews**

You are at a great disadvantage if your competitors have reviews and your landing pages do not. Many website visitors will be looking for proof of your expertise or past performance from reviews –without them, you will find it difficult to convince visitors to use your products or services.

There are many credible third-party review sites like Trustpilot and Feefo and for a small monthly fee, you can collect customer reviews. This will be a great investment for your business.

**Have an 'About Us' page**

Many of your visitors will be looking for an 'About Us' page to learn more about your business before they decide to trade with you. It still amazes me that I find many sites don't have an 'about' page and this is one of the most basic features to add.

Having the 'about' page visible from any of your landing pages will make it easy for your visitors to learn about your business. After reading and gaining more confidence about you, they will return to the landing page to complete a conversion.

## Add a contact form

A contact form is a must if you want to turn visitors into leads. People are more likely to contact you if you have a well-designed, targeted form on your landing page.

It's especially important for mobile visitors who can fill out the form quickly and move on to whatever else they need to do.

Of course, you should have a separate contact page for visitors who want to use that, however, including the form on the landing page will help boost user experience and conversions.

## Have a 'Thank You' page

It's better to have a 'thank you' page for your contact form than an in-line simple thank you message. A thank you page helps to reduce bounce rates for your website and increases overall visitor experience.

You can also use the thank you page to set expectations for your visitor as to when you will get back to them. This is more difficult with a message which will normally just say 'thank you for contacting us. We will contact you shortly'.

Again, with a thank you page you can promote other areas of your website and even a white paper download or eBook, which they can read to learn more about your business.

Finally, a thank you page makes tracking your Google Ads traffic a lot easier. With an in-line message, you would have to set up event tracking, which can be tricky to do at the best of times. With the thank you page, all you need is the URL which you will use to set up goal tracking in Google Analytics and track your PPC traffic easily.

**Update your footer**

Your footer represents the end of the line for your landing page visitor. They have read your content and reached the bottom of the page, but are not sure what to do next.

This is where you can promote other pages on your website by adding links to those pages. You can also add a newsletter signup or a contact form to make it easy for them to make contact.

## Auction Insights Analysis

The Auction Insights Report is a report showing you a list of competitors and how your ads and keywords are performing compared to theirs.

You can see this report in the Campaigns tab or Ad Groups tab in your campaign. Viewing it at the campaign level shows you the competitor metrics for the whole campaign and viewing it at the ad group level shows metrics for that particular group.

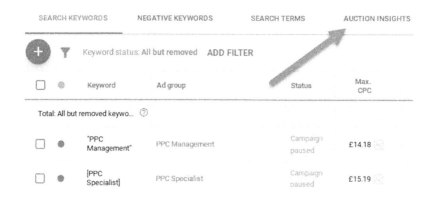

This report can be also accessed from the keywords tab and shows the metrics and stats for the keywords in your campaign or ad group.

The diagram shows competitors in rows and yours appears as 'You'. Next to each competitor you'll see metrics revealing how their ads are performing in relation to yours.

| Display URL domain | ↓ Impression share | Overlap rate | Position above rate |
|---|---|---|---|
| You | 73.70% | — | — |
| wordstream.com | 24.35% | 29.84% | 45.87% |
| linkedin.com | 24.11% | 28.46% | 59.24% |
| keel-over.com | 19.07% | 22.85% | 55.75% |
| click.co.uk | 13.14% | 17.07% | 13.17% |
| pushgroup.co.uk | 11.02% | 12.90% | 32.77% |

For example, 'Top of page rate' shows how often your ad was shown at the top of the page in the search results. So if it's showing as 70%, then 70% of the time your ads were at the top. Or if another advertiser has 63% top of page rate this means their ad was at the top 63% of the time over your ads in the auction.

## Update Bidding Strategy

Google Ads bid management is an essential part of campaign management. From the time you launch your first campaign to managing multiple campaigns, you'll need a strategy to make your advertising a success.

You'll need to decide whether you'll use individual or portfolio bid strategies. You'll also need to decide which bid strategy to use at different stages of your advertising.

Here are three tips to help you with your bid management:

## Have a campaign goal

To set the right Google Ads bids and manage them effectively, you need to have a goal. Your campaign should be set up to achieve that goal and your bid strategy can help.

Some common goals include increasing clicks, impressions, conversions and conversion value, and views. There's at least one bid strategy to help you achieve each of these goals.

To increase clicks, for example, you can use Maximise Clicks. This bid strategy tries to get you as many clicks as possible for your Google Ads budget and sets the bids automatically.

To increase impressions you can use a bid strategy like Target Search Page Location. With this automated bid strategy, your bids will be set up to get you the top position on the first page, or anywhere on the first page of search results.

### Start with maximise clicks

Maximise Clicks is a good bidding strategy to start with. As an automated bid strategy, it does the heavy lifting for you and takes the guesswork out of bidding.

Maximise Clicks is ideal to start using for the following reasons:

- If you're new to Google Ads and have little or no experience with bidding strategies.

- If you're not sure exactly how much to bid for your keywords or placements.

- When you're only interested in increasing web traffic.

- You don't have time to spend monitoring and updating individual CPC bids and are willing to allow Google Ads to update them automatically.

- You want to reach your Google Ads advertising budget consistently.

## Automated or manual bidding

Automated and Manual bidding are the two bidding types in Google Ads. Each has bidding strategies you can use to promote your products or services.

There are 7 automated bid strategies and some of the popular ones are Maximise Clicks and Maximise Conversions. There's only one manual bidding strategy and that's Manual CPC.

Automated strategies set bids for you automatically based on click, conversion, impression, and position goals in the auction results. This can save you a lot of time and you can focus on other areas of your account.

However, you can quickly lose control in managing your bids and it can prove expensive if not handled correctly.

Manual CPC gives you the greatest control because you get to decide on the bids. The benefit is that you decide on what you pay for each click and don't leave it to Google Ads to decide.

The disadvantage of this strategy is that it can be time consuming and ineffective. You're also likely to lose out on opportunities, which an automated bid strategy would pick up quickly.

## Summary

In week 4 we looked at some of the more advanced features in Google Ads. We've explored the quality of your campaign by looking at keyword quality scores, landing page experience and how you can improve these.

We've also covered the Auction Insights report, a report that you should familiarise yourself with and regularly check to see how you are performing against other advertisers. We looked at how you can access it and what it tells us about the metrics for each advertiser, including your ads.

We have also had a look at updating your Bid Strategy when you've run your ads for a while and have more data to choose a more effective strategy.

# Conclusion

That concludes the setup of your account and campaign. By now you should have a fully optimised campaign sure to result in effective results. Follow these steps to create more campaigns in your account and to manage and optimise your ads and keywords.

The Google Support team is available if you have any questions about your, account, campaign, or ads. You can reach them by email, chat, and phone.

**Google Ads Support:**
**Email, chat and phone**

From time to time you may need to contact Google support if you have a query. There are three main ways to do this: phone, chat, and email. Phone support is often the most ideal and is fast, which means you can get your query resolved quickly. This is often best when you want a quick answer to your problem and you need to speak to someone. Google offers a free phone number and you can find this in the Help section of your account.

Email is best if you want to keep a record of your communication with the Google support team.

## Disapproved ads

It's possible that when you first set up your ads and they go through the review process that they will come back as disapproved. This may happen even when your ads and website are not violating any Google Ads policies.

If this happens you should check the status section next to the Ad to find out what the problem is.

Unfortunately, the status column will not provide personalised information on how to fix the disapproval. Google can be a bit vague here, so you may need to conduct a complete review of your ads or website to work out how to fix the disapproved ad. You can also contact the support team for additional help.

# Acknowledgements

First I'd like to thank God Almighty for making this book possible. Thanks to my parents Albert and Judith and my wife Nyarie, without whom this project would not be a success.

And I thank all those who contributed to this work including my editor, graphic designer, and the thousands of clients I've worked with over the years in one way or another.

# Glossary

This information has been gathered from the Google Support section and you can find out more here https://support.google.com/google-ads/answer/2401634?hl=en-GB&ref_topic=24937

**Ad formats** - Visual enhancements to search ads that more prominently display information about your business, such as a phone number, or your website's domain in the headline. These enhancements, which often appear in ads above search results, can include additional content from your website or relevant third-party content. You can add these enhancements manually or they can be added by the Google Ads automated formatting systems. The most common types of ad format are ad extensions. Some examples of ad extensions include location annotations (which attach your business address to your ads) and sitelinks (which include additional links to other pieces of relevant content from additional pages within your site).

**Ad extensions** - A feature that shows extra business information with your ad, like an address, phone number, shop rating or more web page links.

**Ad group** - is a grouping of one or more ads that share similar targets. An ad group also contains one or more keywords that triggers your ad when people search for your product or service on Google. Each campaign is made up of one or more ad groups and you should separate each group by product or service type.

**Ad Rank** - is a value that is used to determine your ad position (where your ad is shown on a page relative to other ads) and whether your ads will show at all. It is calculated using your bid amount, your ad quality, the Ad Rank thresholds, the competitiveness of an auction and many other factors.

**Ad position** - The order in which your ad appears on a page in relation to other ads. For example, an ad position of '1' means that your ad has the highest position on the page relative to other ads of the same type. It doesn't necessarily mean that your ad is above the search results. If there are no ads above the search results, then it means that your ad is the first ad shown beneath search results. Ad position is determined by a formula called Ad Rank that gives your ad a score based on your bid, the quality of your ads and landing page, the Ad Rank thresholds, the context of the person's search and the expected impact of extensions and other ad formats. So even if your competition bids more than you, you can still win a higher position – at a lower price – with highly relevant keywords and ads.

**Ad Preview and Diagnosis Tool -** A tool in your account that helps you to identify why your ad or ad extension might not be appearing. The tool also shows a preview of a Google search result page for a specific term. This helps you see which ads and extensions are appearing for your keyword. When you enter a search term and other criteria like language and location, the tool will tell you whether your ad is eligible to appear in that situation. The Ad Preview and Diagnosis tool suggests search term auto-completions as you type. Suggestions come from keywords with impressions in your account, and are ordered by volume.

**Budget** - this is the average amount that you are willing to spend in your campaign each day. You set an average daily budget for each campaign and on days when your ads are popular you will spend up to twice your average daily budget so you don't miss out on valuable clicks. But don't worry, over a course of a course, you won't be charged more than your average daily budget times the average number of days in a month (30.4 days).

**Campaign** - is a collection of ad groups (Ads and keywords) that share a budget, location targets, language settings, goals, ad schedules and other settings. Your account can have one or many campaigns and each campaign will have one or more ad groups and you can create campaigns for different locations or with different budgets.

**Click** - a click is when someone clicks your ad, like on the blue headline of a text ad. Clicks can help you understand how well your ads are appealing to people that see them. It's important to note that a click is counted even if the person doesn't reach your website, like when it is unavailable. And this is why you may see a difference between the number of clicks on your ad and the number of visitors to your website.

**Click Through Rate (CTR)** - A ratio showing how often people who see your ad end up clicking it. Click-through rate (CTR) can be used to gauge how well your keywords and ads are performing. CTR is the number of clicks that your ad receives divided by the number of times your ad is shown: clicks ÷ impressions = CTR. For example, if you had 5 clicks and 100 impressions, then your CTR would be 5%.

**Conversion rate** - The average number of conversions per ad interaction, shown as a percentage. Conversion rates are calculated by simply taking the number of conversions and dividing that by the number of total ad interactions that can be tracked to a conversion during the same time period. For example, if you had 50 conversions from 1,000 interactions, your conversion rate would be 5%, since 50 ÷ 1,000 = 5%.

**Google Analytics** - A free Google product that provides in-depth reporting on how people use your website. You can use Google Analytics to learn what people do after clicking your ads. Google Analytics shows you how people found your site and how they explored it. From this information, you can get ideas for how to enhance your website.

**Google Display Network** - Google sites like YouTube, Blogger and Gmail, plus thousands of partnering websites across the Internet.

**Google forwarding number** - Google forwarding number is a unique phone number from Google that can be used in your ads to help track calls to your business. It can be used by turning on call reporting in your account settings.

**Google Search Network** - Google search results pages, other Google sites such as Maps and Shopping, and search sites that partner with Google to show ads.

**Impressions** - How often your ad is shown. An impression is counted each time your ad is shown on a search result page or other site on the Google Network. Each time that your ad appears on Google or the Google Network, it's counted as one impression.

**Keywords** - Words or phrases describing your product or service that you choose to help determine when and where your ad can appear. The keywords that you choose are used to show your ads to people. Select high-quality, relevant keywords for your ad campaign to help you reach only the most interested people, who are more likely to become your customers. When someone searches on Google, your ad could be eligible to appear based on the similarity of your keywords to the person's search terms.

**Keyword Planner tool** - Keyword Planner is a tool that provides keyword ideas and traffic estimates to help you build a Search Network campaign. Search for keyword and ad groups ideas based on terms that describe your product or service, your website or a product category related to what you're advertising. You can also enter or upload a list of keywords. And you can multiply two or more lists of keywords to create a new list that combines your keywords.

**Landing page** - The web page where people end up after they click your ad. The URL of this page is usually the same as your ad's final URL. For each ad, you specify a final URL to determine the landing page where people are taken when they click your ad.

**Landing page experience** - A measure that Google Ads uses to estimate how relevant and useful your website's landing page will be to people who click your ad. Landing pages with higher ratings are usually well organised and have text that relates to a person's search terms.

**Location targeting** - A setting that lets you choose your target locations to contact your customers. For each ad campaign, you can select locations where you want your ad to be shown.

Location targeting then allows your ads to appear for people in those locations.

**Manual payments** - A payment setting in which you pay for your advertising costs before your ads run. Then, as your ads run, your costs are deducted from the payment that you've made.

**Match Types (Keyword)** - Settings for each keyword that help control how closely the keyword needs to match a person's search term in order to trigger your ad. Each keyword uses a matching option to help control which searches should trigger your ad to show. You can choose one or more matching options for a keyword. If you don't specify a particular matching option, keywords are considered as broad match. The other three match types are modified broad, phrase and exact match.

**Negative keyword** - A type of keyword that prevents your ad from being triggered by a certain word or phrase. Your ads aren't shown to anyone who is searching for that phrase. This is also known as a negative match. For example, when you add "free" as a negative keyword to your campaign or ad group, you tell Google Ads not to show your ad for any searches containing the term "free". On the Display Network, your ad is less likely to appear on a site when your negative keywords match the site's content.

**Quality Score (QS)** - Quality Score is a keyword metric that measures the quality and relevance of your keywords and ads. It is one of the factors that determine your Ad Rank, with the other being your bid. The three main Quality Score factors are landing page experience, ad relevance and expected click through rate and each of these will have a performance status of Below Average, Average or Above Average. Each keyword will have a score between 1 to 10 and you should always aim to achieve high quality scores by working on one of the three factors listed above.

**Remarketing** - Remarketing is a feature that lets you customise your display ads campaign for people who have previously visited your site, and tailor your bids and ads (using dynamic remarketing) to these visitors when they browse the web and use apps.

**URL** - the page on your website that people reach when they click your ad. This is also known as Final URL and you add one to each text ad that you create.

# Author Biography

Mike Ncube is the Founder and CEO of a digital marketing agency and is passionate about Google Ads and digital marketing.

He has been a Google Partner since the Partner programs inception and he is a regular contributor to industry websites such as Search Engine Watch and ClickZ.

Mike was born and raised in Zimbabwe, Southern Africa, in a family of 9. He moved to California, USA, as a youth to pursue his studies and then later moved to the United Kingdom where he has lived for 20 years. He currently resides in the UK with his wife and they enjoy travelling.

Mike Ncube

Web: www.mikencube.co.uk
Email: info@mikencube.co.uk
Twitter: https://twitter.com/mikencube
LinkedIn: https://www.linkedin.com/in/mikencube/

CPSIA information can be obtained
at www.ICGtesting.com
Printed in the USA
BVHW040149281020
591990BV00017B/473